THE SILENCE THEY WROTE FOR ME

Abigal Muchecheti

THE SILENCE THEY WROTE FOR ME

A Black Disabled Woman's Fight Against Institutional Erasure

Disability Studies
Collection Editor
Damian Mellifont

LPp

First published in 2025 by Lived Places Publishing

British Library Cataloguing in Publication Data
A CIP record for this book is available from the British Library.

ISBN: 9781915271129 (pbk)
ISBN: 9781915271143 (ePDF)
ISBN: 9781915271136 (ePUB)

Cover design by Fiachra McCarthy
Book design by Rachel Trolove of Twin Trail Design
Typeset by Newgen Publishing, UK

Lived Places Publishing
P.O. Box 1845
47 Echo Avenue
Miller Place, NY 11764

www.livedplacespublishing.com

To every psychiatric survivor who whispered their truth into a system that refused to hear it, this book is yours. You are not invisible. You are not broken. You are the archive, the witness, the theorist.

To my son, Farai Nigel, whose name means joy, whose presence reminds me why we fight to build worlds that don't pathologise feeling. May you never inherit silence as protection. You are the reason I write.

To my husband, Phillip – thank you for holding me through the tremors, for reading the words I couldn't yet speak, and for standing beside me as I tore open the truths hidden in white coats and locked doors.

To my mother, gone but never absent – your strength lives in these pages, in the language I reclaimed when they tried to strip it away. I am here because you survived. I write because you did not.

Some of us were never meant to survive. Still here we are, writing from the after. Adapted from Audre Lorde and the voices that lived beyond the ward.

Abstract

This book is a fugitive document. *The Silence they wrote for me* is part lived experience, part manifesto, and part abolitionist intervention. It interrogates the psychiatric system in the UK as a site of racialised, gendered, and epistemic violence, particularly under the use of Section 2 of the Mental Health Act 1983. Drawing from five years of participatory action research and lived experience, this book centres Black women and racialised survivors whose voices are often silenced under the guise of care.

Rather than seeking reform, it enacts refusal. Through testimonial circles, dream mapping, sousveillance, and insurgent storytelling, this book offers abolitionist blueprints for relational mental health justice. Each chapter excavates violence but also gestures towards healing – towards the world that must be built in psychiatry's ruins. *The Silence they wrote for me* is not about inclusion in the system. It is about survival beyond it.

Key words

Psychiatric abolition, Section 2, Black women, Racialised trauma, Mental health justice, Survivor testimony, Epistemic violence, Abolitionist futures, Carceral care, UK psychiatry

Contents

Content warning

This book contains personal accounts and analyses of psychiatric detention, forced treatment, institutional racism, and systemic abuse under the UK Mental Health Act. It includes references to loss, grief, restraint, surveillance, and gaslighting within clinical environments.

These narratives are not included to shock. They are offered as truth-telling and testimony, as tools for abolition, not consumption. Reader care and community grounding are encouraged.

Learning objectives

By the end of this book, readers should be able to:

1. Understand and critically assess the racialised and gendered dynamics of psychiatric detention in the UK, with a focus on how Black women and racialised individuals are disproportionately harmed under Section 2 of the Mental Health Act.
2. Recognise the concept of epistemic violence and how psychiatric systems erase, discredit, or silence the knowledge and experiences of survivors, especially those marked as "foreign," "non-compliant," or "too coherent."
3. Examine the intersections of carceral logics, mental health care, and structural racism, particularly as enacted through uniforms, surveillance, ward hierarchies, and diagnostic practices.
4. Interrogate the myth of neutrality in psychiatric spaces, exploring how power operates through the presence of white male and institutional gazes ("The Men in the Room") and through the flattening of difference ("Levelled").
5. Engage with the methodology of refusal as both a political stance and a writing practice, including testimonial circles, dream mapping, sousveillance, and insurgent storytelling.

Introduction

> You are not unwell; you are ungovernable.
>
> Survivor testimony, 2022

This book is both testimony and theory. It emerges from the ruins of psychiatric institutions in the UK, places where the line between care and control collapses and where racialised, disabled, and non-conforming bodies are held not to be healed but to be corrected, sedated, or silenced.

I began writing from within the walls of a psychiatric ward. I was detained under Section 2 of the Mental Health Act 1983, diagnosed and labelled in ways that sought to render my grief pathological, my knowledge delusional, and my presence disruptive. But even there, in a place designed to mute resistance, I wrote. This book is the result of that writing – an attempt to hold memory and meaning in a system structured around forgetting and erasure.

Methodological refusals: Researching from within

This is not neutral research. It is insurgent research, a refusal to produce knowledge for institutional consumption and a commitment to epistemologies born of survival. This book draws on five years of participatory action research (PAR) conducted in collaboration with psychiatric survivors, abolitionist organisers, and care workers across England.

The work is grounded in Black feminist theory, disability justice, and carceral geography and uses methods shaped by refusal, relational accountability, and radical imagination:

- Testimonial Circles: Inspired by Patricia Hill Collins's "kitchen table epistemologies," these were survivor-led spaces not just for storytelling but for analysis, grief work, and politicisation.
- Sousveillance Practices: Participants shared encrypted documentation – audio recordings, visual artefacts, texts – to collectively archive what the system refused to acknowledge.
- Dream Mapping: Through speculative sketches, poetry, and spatial dreaming, survivors envisioned abolitionist care beyond the psychiatric state.
- Co-Analysis: Interpretations were shaped through dialogue. No contribution was published without consent. Some remain unpublished as a result of participants choice.

Participants were mostly Black and racialised women, many of whom had experienced Section 2 or Section 3 detainment. Their ages ranged from early 20s to late 60s. Interviews were conducted post-discharge in places chosen by the participants: kitchens, parks, WhatsApp voice notes, and poetry groups. No one was interviewed inside a hospital. My refusal to do so was central to the ethics of this work.

My own experience stands apart: I wrote *from within* the ward. The book begins there – with my own letters, notes, and observations – before moving outward to include other voices, other refusals, and other strategies of survival.

Book structure

Introduction: Methodological refusals and writing from within

This book begins by rejecting institutional demands for neutrality and academic distance. Instead, it embraces a method of *writing from within* that is grounded in lived experience and narrated through fragments, refusals, and testimonies. This introduction outlines the book's theoretical commitments to Black feminist thought, disability justice, and decolonial epistemologies. It positions the work as a fugitive archive that is rooted in care but unafraid to indict.

Chapter 1: The body they feared

Containment, diagnosis, and writing from the ward

This chapter introduces the racialised, gendered body as a threat in psychiatric institutions – it is both feared and disciplined. Through letters, ward notes, and narrative fragments, it reveals how psychiatric "care" becomes a form of carceral control. The body is sedated, surveilled, and restrained – not because it is unstable, but because it refuses to conform.

Chapter 2: Locked spaces, locked voice

Language, muteness, and institutional control

Silence is imposed and internalised. This chapter explores how institutional practices, from isolation to overmedication, systematically strip patients of their voice. Women learn to self-censor, knowing that coherence can be misread as mania and grief as risk. Drawing on Foucault (1977), Fanon (1967), and participant accounts, it theorises silence as both coercive and strategic.

Chapter 3: Violence in uniforms

Coercion by staff, security, and police in psychiatric institutions

This chapter interrogates how uniforms – medical and security staff and police uniforms – become vessels of psychiatric force. From forced injections to physical restraints, it documents how state violence operates within therapeutic settings. What is called "protection" is often indistinguishable from punishment. Testimonies trace the fear, humiliation, and physical trauma inflicted under the guise of care.

Chapter 4: The men in the room

Patriarchy, power, and gendered violence in psychiatric care

Here, the analysis turns towards gender. Drawing on Oyěwùmí (1997), Fanon (1967, and Wynter (2003), this chapter explores how African and racialised men are positioned as institutional enforcers. Their masculinity is produced through proximity to colonial authority, often at the expense of vulnerable women. Psychiatric masculinity emerges as a performance of domination – legitimised through force, rewarded through control.

Chapter 5: Estranged minds: Migration, madness, and institutional abandonment

This chapter examines how immigrant women, especially those without visitors, language support, or cultural familiarity, are cast as hyper-pathologised and structurally alone. Their foreignness becomes evidence of madness. Drawing on diasporic feminisms (Brah, Spivak, Anzaldúa), it exposes how displacement, untranslatability, and cultural misrecognition compound psychiatric harm. These women are not just patients, they are perceived as lost.

Chapter 6: Epistemic violence

Silencing, pathologising, and denial of knowledge

This chapter analyses how psychiatric institutions erase the knowledge that comes from survival. Black women's spiritual, cultural, and intellectual expressions are framed as delusion or defiance. It interrogates how Western psychiatry defines what counts as insight and how those definitions silence the very people they claim to help.

Chapter 7: Levelled

Institutional flattening of memory, identity, and agency

Here, the book reveals how identity is stripped through institutional life. Creativity, language, cultural memory, and even clothing become regulated. Women are rendered flat, not because they lack personality but because the system cannot tolerate difference. Flattening is misread as healing and conformity is misread as recovery.

Chapter 8: Exiting but not free

Surveillance, stigma, and systemic abandonment post-discharge

Discharge is not freedom. This chapter documents the continuation of psychiatric surveillance in therapy, employment, education, and family life. Women describe being disbelieved, over-policed, and discredited long after the ward doors closed. Recovery is conditional. Wellness is mistrusted. Diagnosis becomes a haunting.

Chapter 9: What I could not say in the ward

Memory, love, rage, and the unspoken truths

This is the book's most intimate chapter. It gathers the fragments, the things participants dared not say until it was too late. Rage, longing, shame, erotic memory, ancestral visitation, and inner clarity all emerge. What psychiatry called symptoms, this chapter reads as forms of knowing.

Chapter 10: Building otherwise

CARE: A decolonial framework for abolitionist mental health

This final chapter offers a future. Through the CARE framework – *Collective refusal, Accountability, Relational infrastructures, Emergence* – it outlines a vision for mental health that is rooted in abolition, community care, and relational healing. This is not reform. This is what survival makes possible – the right to live otherwise.

Epilogue: When silence becomes a weapon, so does the word

Closing the door on reform, opening the path to insurgent healing

This closing reflects on silence as resistance and language as reclamation. It refuses institutional redemption, and instead it centres the wisdom of survivors and the necessity of building in the aftermath. To speak is not to forgive, it is to continue.

References

Anzaldúa, G. (1987). Borderlands/La Frontera: The New Mestiza. San Francisco: Aunt Lute Books.

Brah, A. (1996). Cartographies of Diaspora: Contesting Identities. London: Routledge.

Fanon, F. (1967). Black Skin, White Masks. Translated by C. L. Markmann. New York: Grove Press.

Foucault, M. (1977). *Discipline and punish: The birth of the prison.* Translated by A. Sheridan. New York: Pantheon Books.

Oyěwùmí, O. (1997). The Invention of Women: Making an African Sense of Western Gender Discourses. Minneapolis: University of Minnesota Press.

Spivak, G. C. (1988). 'Can the Subaltern Speak?', in Nelson, C. and Grossberg, L. (eds.) Marxism and the Interpretation of Culture. Urbana: University of Illinois Press, pp. 271–313.

Survivor letter Collective (2021).

Wynter, S. (2003). 'Unsettling the Coloniality of Being/ Power/Truth/Freedom: Towards the Human, After Man, Its Overrepresentation—An Argument', CR: The New Centennial Review, 3(3), pp. 257–337.

Introduction: Methodological Refusals and Writing from Within

This book was not written from the outside looking in. It was written from within the machinery of harm from hospital corridors where silence was enforced, from the waiting rooms where speech became suspicion, and from the long aftermath of being written about, rather than written with. The Silence They Wrote for Me emerges from that inside space, one marked by surveillance, medicalisation, and the quiet undoing of selfhood. To write from within is to refuse the safety of abstraction. It is to speak from the cracks of a system that names pain as pathology, and to turn those cracks into method.

Methodological refusal, in this sense, is not simply an academic stance but a survival strategy. It is the decision to write without permission from institutional ethics boards, disciplinary expectations, or the voyeuristic demands of the reader. Refusal here means writing against the grain of what counts as knowledge, what counts as recovery, and who is deemed coherent enough to be believed. It is a way of claiming authorship over the narrative that psychiatry, bureaucracy, and academia sought to overwrite.

This book does not present findings; it bears witness. It does not offer closure; it dwells in the unfinished. Writing from within means sitting with the textures of silence — the bureaucratic, the clinical, the intimate and asking how they accumulate into structural violence. It means tracing the contours of a body made unrecognisable by systems that claim to protect. And it means reassembling that body through fragments of memory, theory, and resistance.

What follows is not a linear account but a series of reckonings. Each chapter unravels how the architecture of care becomes the architecture of control, how silence is demanded yet weaponised, and how the very act of narrating one's experience becomes both testimony and trespass. To write from within is to insist that those who have been institutionalised, dismissed, or erased are not objects of study but theorists of their own condition.

In writing this book, I do not seek to heal the institution or make its violence more understandable. My aim is to make its violence visible to expose the banality through which harm is normalised, paperwork becomes punishment, and silence becomes policy. This is not a book of redemption. It is a book of refusal, of quiet defiance, and of reclaiming language from the margins of coherence.

1
The body they feared Containment, diagnosis, and writing from the ward

The doors did not slam, but they closed behind me with the slow, final certainty of something that no longer needed to announce itself. I had entered a hospital, but what I found was an institution of control. From the colourless walls to the humming buzz of surveillance systems, everything spoke the language of containment. Nothing about that space said healing. It said management. It said: you are now someone we must monitor.

They took my name first – then my clothes, then my voice.

This spatial choreography of control is not incidental, it is historical. The very design of psychiatric spaces reflects what Foucault (1977; p. 170) described as the rise of disciplinary institutions: sites where power operates through observation, categorisation, and normalisation. Mental health wards, like prisons and schools, function as "enclosures" in which surveillance is continuous and the individual is made legible through a regime of notes, diagnoses, and files. These are spaces that extract compliance under the guise of care.

This book is grounded in critical autoethnography and informed by disability justice, Black feminist theory, and carceral geography. Chapter 1 draws from my own documented experience of psychiatric institutionalisation, using excerpts from contemporaneous letters, observation notes, and recordings. All identifying information has been anonymised. The events described are not anecdotal but are situated within patterns evidenced by broader research, public data, and the structural realities of UK mental health systems (Boylorn, 2016; Ellis et al., 2011).

In the early moments of my admission, I saw myself becoming a stranger to those around me and eventually to myself. I was not greeted as someone in distress or someone deserving of care. I was read. My body was read. My skin, my gender, my tone, and my posture were all misinterpreted through the diagnostic gaze that pathologises the Black female body before it ever speaks. I did not need to act angry to be labelled as such. I only needed to exist within a body that institutions have long feared, silenced, and over-disciplined.

This chapter traces how the institutionalisation of Black women in psychiatric care is not simply about health but about histories. It is about power and the cultural production of pathology. As bell hooks (1981) and Collins (2000) remind us, institutions do not merely reflect dominant ideologies, they reproduce them. Psychiatry, in its institutional form, often becomes a mechanism for managing what society refuses to care for: the inconvenient, the unruly, the raced and gendered other.

Institutions as sites of racial control

Psychiatric institutions in the UK do not operate in a vacuum. They are historical artefacts shaped by empire, eugenics, racial science, and carceral logic. As Fanon (1967, made clear, colonial psychiatry was never about understanding the mental health of the colonised. It was a disciplinary tool, deployed to suppress resistance, pathologise defiance, and justify the paternalistic control of Black bodies. That legacy persists.

Mental health facilities, particularly those used for compulsory detainment, have long mirrored prison architectures – what Foucault (1977) calls the "carceral continuum." They are spaces of control dressed up in the language of care. These institutions function as what Alexander (2010) terms the new racial caste system: they are not overtly exclusionary but are quietly devastating through disproportionate surveillance, detention, and sedation of racialised subjects.

Gilmore (2007) extends this logic through her theory of carceral geography, describing how institutions that spatially separate and constrain certain bodies also produce social death. In this view, psychiatric wards are not simply medical spaces. They are racialised technologies of power where some lives are routinely deemed unmanageable and thus unworthy of autonomy.

Black women in particular are disproportionately caught within these systems – not because we are inherently more unwell, but because our emotional expressions are interpreted through a framework of threat. As Davis (1981) notes, institutions historically feared the political potential of angry or grieving Black women. That fear has not disappeared. It has simply become medicalised.

When I entered the ward, I felt the full force of this history. The space itself communicated mistrust. Windowless corridors. Observation windows. Alarms on staff belts. It was a choreography of containment where even kindness felt scripted. Butler (2009) reminds us that some lives are seen as less grievable. In the ward, my presence was treated as threat mitigation, not care. I was already outside the realm of empathy.

I had not arrived in the ward voluntarily. My husband had called NHS 111 after I had not been sleeping for several days. I was exhausted, not violent, but I was sectioned under the Mental Health Act. From the outset, I was under forced control. Consent was never part of the equation.

These institutions, framed by medical neutrality, often reproduce the same logics of containment found in prisons, schools, and immigration detention centres, especially when it comes to the treatment of Black women. We are not admitted. We are processed. And once inside, we are marked not by what we say or do, but by what we represent: risk.

I've described earlier what it meant to be sectioned – for exhaustion, not violence. But the deeper violence came after.

I was detained under the Mental Health Act not for harm, but for depletion, and from that moment, control replaced care. There was no language of consent, only procedures of risk management. The environment made it clear: I was not to be trusted. Narrow corridors without windows, shatterproof glass panels, staff radios clipped to belts. Every detail choreographed surveillance over support. Even kindness, when it appeared, arrived as part of protocol.

As Butler (2009) reminds us, not all lives are equally grievable. Inside the ward, I was not treated as someone in pain, but as someone to be contained. Especially as a Black woman, I was not admitted into care – I was processed through it. What marked me wasn't my behaviour, but what I embodied: unpredictability, deviance, threat. These institutions may claim neutrality, but they often mimic the structures of prisons, schools, and border regimes – spaces where racialised bodies are managed, not understood.

Who gets detained? Who decides?

The decision to detain someone under the Mental Health Act is rarely framed as racialised, yet the statistical disparities are irrefutable. Black people in the UK are over four times more likely to be detained under the Act than white people. Black women compared to White women, specifically, are disproportionately subject to compulsory admission, restraint, and forced medication, frequently through police involvement rather than therapeutic referral (Care Quality Commission, 2021; Fernando, 2017). These disproportionate rates are not the result of random clinical judgement, but rather reflect systemic practices embedded in colonial legacies, racial hierarchies, and gendered logics of social control.

Who gets detained – and who decides – cannot be understood outside the sociopolitical apparatus that constructs risk as racialised. As Roberts (1997) argues, Black bodies are hyper-surveilled and disproportionately punished across welfare, criminal justice, and healthcare systems, which treat Black women not as subjects of care but as objects of discipline. The psychiatric gaze does not merely observe – it classifies, labels, and confines. The very notion of "risk" is a racialised and gendered construct, produced within what Crenshaw (1989) theorised as intersecting axes of oppression.

The image of the "madwoman" is not new, but when applied to a Black woman, it becomes a dangerous amalgam of colonial phobia and contemporary institutional fear. A Black woman who cries is hysterical. A Black woman who questions is oppositional. A Black woman who refuses sedation is aggressive. These misreadings are not clinical errors; they are cultural scripts, enacted through the bureaucratic apparatus of mental health services.

Professionals – psychiatrists, crisis teams, social workers, police – operate with considerable discretion. Yet their discretion is shaped by institutional cultures and racialised scripts. Diagnostic labels are not handed out in neutral terms; they reflect the ideologies of those empowered to make them. The designation of a Black woman as "non-compliant" or "lacking insight" functions as both a silencing tool and a justification for greater control. As Davis (1981) and hooks (1992) remind us, the social order depends on managing the perceived deviance of Black women's affective lives.

What appears to be a clinical decision is often the endpoint of a racialised chain of assumptions. The cumulative outcome is not just a misreading, it is also a material consequence: overmedication, isolation, restraint, institutionalisation. This is what Collins (2000) identifies as the enduring legacy of controlling images: the Angry Black Woman, the unbreakable matriarch, the deviant. These narratives shape how we are seen, how we are treated, and how we are silenced. They determine who is deemed worthy of gentleness and who is punished for not being small enough to care for. These narratives shape the way that care is withheld or administered. They determine who is deemed worthy of gentleness and who is not.

Diagnostic violence: A routine scene

The violence of diagnosis does not always arrive with sirens or restraint. It is often banal, papered over with administrative language and clinical efficiency. Yet its effects are profound. Every morning, we lined up for medication – an orchestrated ritual that resembled order more than care. I watched as some patients received single pills in plastic cups. Mine was a cocktail. I asked what each one was for. The nurse looked annoyed: "It's in your notes. We've explained this before." But I hadn't been told.

This denial of knowledge was part of a larger apparatus of control. Asking too many questions flagged you as disruptive. Wanting clarity positioned you as oppositional. Each act of self-advocacy became a threat to the fragile balance the ward tried to maintain.

I was monitored constantly – not only for safety, but to ensure compliance. When I once refused a new prescription and asked to speak with the psychiatrist first, the response wasn't dialogue. Instead, a note appeared in my file: "Patient oppositional, displays low insight." In that moment, my insistence on understanding my own treatment was pathologised. What should have been seen as reasonable hesitation was framed as defiance, a failure to submit, rather than a right to ask questions.

That note became a cipher. It outlived my protests and explained away my discomfort. It followed me from shift to shift. Staff who had never spoken to me treated me as a behavioural risk. A single comment shaped every future interaction. There was no room for my version of the story.

As Foucault (1977) argues, power in institutional spaces operates not only through force but through the production of truth. Diagnosis is not a neutral reflection of symptoms, but a statement of authority, a claim about the nature of a person that becomes legible within institutional logic. Hartman (1997) calls these moments "scenes of subjection": routine, rehearsed acts that render Black subjects objects of control. These are not exceptional events; they are the daily grammar of institutional power.

Beyond Foucault and Hartman, Roberts (2016) and Hansen et al. (2013) have shown how diagnosis operates as a form of social regulation, marking out those whose distress challenges normative scripts of productivity, civility, and whiteness. Hansen's work on structural competency critiques how psychiatric education trains clinicians to overlook structural violence while focusing narrowly on patient compliance. Meanwhile, Roberts reminds us that diagnostic categories, particularly those disproportionately applied to Black women, serve to inscribe racial hierarchy through medical language.

Disability theorist Davis (2006) critiques the normate of those presumed able, rational, and stable as the silent baseline against which others are judged and pathologised. Within psychiatric institutions, this baseline becomes weaponised through diagnostic protocols that misread difference as deviance. The racialised patient who deviates from the expected behavioural script becomes a clinical problem rather than a person in distress.

In the psychiatric ward, diagnostic violence is cumulative, bureaucratic, and deeply racialised. As Metzl (2009) demonstrates in his analysis of schizophrenia diagnoses in the United States, Black men and women are disproportionately medicalised through the lens of deviance rather than vulnerability, reinforcing racial stereotypes under the guise of clinical objectivity. Similarly, the UK context reflects a racialised logic wherein the psychiatric system does not need overt racism to function repressively; it only requires the continued reproduction of diagnostic practices that silence, pathologise, and erase those deemed disruptive to institutional norms. These diagnostic practices are rooted in what Fanon (1967) identifies as the colonial impulse to control the mind by pathologising the colonised. When diagnostic power intersects with racialised and gendered surveillance, the result is not simply a misunderstanding, but a structure in which certain voices are overwritten before they are ever heard.

It only requires the reproduction of a system where some voices are overwritten before they are ever heard.

What haunts me still is that much of the violence came from staff of colour. Not because they were cruel, but because they were caught. Many of them were working class, underpaid, and oversurveilled themselves. They were expected to manage us with a smile, contain us without escalation, and protect the ward from our questions while managing their own trauma.

Ahmed (2012) reminds us that pointing out institutional problems often turns the whistleblower into the problem. In this system, care staff are the buffer zone between patients and power. They are often the ones carrying out orders but have no space for dissent. Racial capitalism, as Gilmore (2007) notes, recruits the racialised subject to maintain the very institutions that exclude them.

This is structural capture: the transformation of vulnerable workers into agents of harm. Not always intentionally. Often mournfully. They were not villains. But they were not free.

The first letter

That night, I began to write. On the back of a leaflet about crisis recovery, I scrawled the first lines of what would become my survival archive:

> They said I was angry. I was asking. They said I was resistant. I was scared. They said I was unstable. I was unheard.

This is how the record begins. Not theirs. Mine.Writing became a form of resistance. Not the kind that makes headlines, but the kind that keeps you tethered to yourself when everything else is being stripped away. As Lorde (1984) teaches us, our silence will not protect us, but neither will speaking unless we claim the right to be heard. In that moment, I was not simply recording events; I was reclaiming authorship.

Autoethnographic writing in contexts of psychiatric oppression functions not only as catharsis but as an epistemological and political intervention. Ellis and Bochner (2000) describe autoethnography as a method that blurs the boundary between researcher and subject, insisting that lived experience has theoretical weight. Writing thus became a form of what Minh-ha (1989) calls "speaking nearby": not a direct confrontation, but a subversive rewriting of institutional silencing.

This act of documentation is also what Morrison (1992) calls "rememory" – a way of bringing forward the erased. It is a counter-archive to the official file, a refusal to let the institutional record stand as the only narrative. In recording my own truth, I was participating in what Ahmed (2017) terms complaint as feminist pedagogy – speaking from within structures that are hostile to your voice, yet daring to speak anyway.

These letters, scribbled in quiet moments, became my methodology. They are what Kafer (2013) might call crip time: non-linear, interruptive, embodied. They defy the sanitised linearity of progress narratives. They insist that documentation is survival.

Conclusion

This chapter has traced the multiple layers through which psychiatric institutions operate as racialised and gendered technologies of control. By examining diagnostic practices, spatial arrangements, institutional responses, and recorded interactions, we see how Black women are not merely misread, but are systematically dehumanised through clinical language and bureaucratic ritual. What is framed as treatment often functions as containment. What is labelled as care often manifests as coercion.

Using an autoethnographic approach, I have illustrated how institutional responses to distress are mediated by intersecting structures of racism, sexism, ableism, and class inequality. The concept of diagnostic violence which is bureaucratic, cumulative, and racialised illustrates that institutional harm does not always depend on overt acts. It unfolds through the reproduction of medical authority, surveillance, and silence. As such, Black women become both hyper-visible and invisible: watched closely, yet never truly seen.

This chapter has also shown how institutional complicity extends beyond white power structures. Racial capitalism enlists racialised workers into practices of surveillance and control, producing what Gilmore (2007) calls structural capture. The institution shapes everyone within it – patients, staff, and observers – into participants in the management of those it deems deviant.

By anchoring this chapter in Black feminist theory, carceral geography, and disability justice, I locate psychiatric harm not as an aberration but as a patterned outcome. The figure of the "unwell Black woman" is not constructed through symptoms alone but through institutional logic that have always mistrusted her presence, voice, and body.

This is not a call for reform alone. It is a demand for epistemic and institutional accountability. The records kept about me were not only incomplete but were structured to exclude my voice. That is why this chapter insists on naming, documenting, and refusing.

The chapters that follow expand this inquiry into space, silence, complicity, and exile, mapping not only what was done to me but what was made possible by my absence.

Reflexive questions: Reading from within

1. Whose bodies does the institution prepare for, and whose bodies does it control?

Consider how physical and spatial arrangements (e.g. locked doors, observation panels, alarms) reflect broader assumptions about race, gender, and "risk."

2. What images come to mind when you hear the term "unwell?" Who taught you those images?

Reflect on how societal and institutional narratives shape who is seen as ill, dangerous, or in need of control and who is not.

3. When have you witnessed or participated in the silencing of a person's truth through "professional" language or institutional protocol?

Think about how terms like "non-compliant," "aggressive," or "lacking insight" may be used to erase rather than support.

4. How do you read distress when it shows up in Black women? What logic are shaping your response?

Be honest: what assumptions do you make when someone doesn't cry softly or speak gently? How are these shaped by dominant scripts of civility and whiteness?

5. What does it mean to treat documentation as resistance? What stories are missing from the official file, and why?

Consider who gets to write the record, and who is written over. What would it mean to centre survivor archives instead?

References

Ahmed, S. (2012). *On Being Included: Racism and Diversity in Institutional Life*. Durham, Duke University Press.

Ahmed, S. (2017). *Living a Feminist Life*. Durham, NC: Duke University Press.

Alexander, M. (2010). *The New Jim Crow: Mass Incarceration in the Age of Colorblindness*. New York: The New Press.

Boylorn, R. M. (2016). Earning the 'Earned Income Tax Credit': A Black feminist autoethnography. *Critical Race and Whiteness Studies*, 12(2), 1–14.

Butler, J. (2009). *Frames of War: When Is Life Grievable?* London: Verso.

Care Quality Commission (2021). *Monitoring the Mental Health Act in 2019/20*. London: CQC.

Collins, P. H. (2000). *Black Feminist Thought: Knowledge, Consciousness, and the Politics of Empowerment*. 2nd edn. New York: Routledge.

Crenshaw, K. (1989). Demarginalizing the intersection of race and sex: A Black feminist critique of antidiscrimination doctrine. *University of Chicago Legal Forum*, 139–167.

Davis, A. (1981). *Women, Race, & Class*. New York: Random House.

Davis, L. J. (2006). *The Disability Studies Reader*. New York: Routledge.

Ellis, C., Adams, T. E. and Bochner, A. P. (2011). Autoethnography: An overview. *Forum Qualitative Sozialforschung / Forum: Qualitative Social Research*, 12(1), Art. 10.

Ellis, C. and Bochner, A. P. (2000). Autoethnography, personal narrative, reflexivity. In: Denzin, N. K. and Lincoln, Y. S. (eds.) *Handbook of Qualitative Research*. 2nd edn. Thousand Oaks: Sage.

Fanon, F. (1967/1952). *Black Skin, White Masks*. Translated by C. L. Markmann. New York: Grove Press.

Fernando, S. (2017). *Institutional Racism in Psychiatry and Clinical Psychology: Race Matters in Mental Health*. 2nd edn. Cham: Palgrave Macmillan.

Foucault, M. (1977). *Discipline and Punish: The Birth of the Prison*. Translated by A. Sheridan. New York: Vintage.

Gilmore, R. W. (2007). *Golden Gulag: Prisons, Surplus, Crisis, and Opposition in Globalizing California*. Berkeley: University of California Press.

Hansen, H., Metzl, J. and Prather, C. (2013). Structural competency: Theorizing a new medical engagement with stigma and inequality. *Social Science & Medicine*, 103, 126–133.

Hartman, S. V. (1997). *Scenes of Subjection: Terror, Slavery, and Self-Making in Nineteenth-Century America*. Oxford: Oxford University Press.

Hill Collins, P. (2000). *Black Feminist Thought*. 2nd edn. New York: Routledge.

hooks, b. (1981). *Ain't I a Woman: Black Women and Feminism*. Boston: South End Press.

hooks, b. (1992). *Black Looks: Race and Representation*. Boston: South End Press.

Kafer, A. (2013). *Feminist, Queer, Crip*. Bloomington: Indiana University Press.

Lorde, A. (1984). *Sister Outsider: Essays and Speeches*. Berkeley, CA: Crossing Press.

Metzl, J. M. (2009). *The Protest Psychosis: How Schizophrenia Became a Black Disease*. Boston: Beacon Press.

Minh-ha, T. T. (1989). *Woman, Native, Other: Writing Postcoloniality and Feminism*. Bloomington: Indiana University Press.

Morrison, T. (1992). *Beloved*. London: Vintage.

Roberts, D. (1997). *Killing the Black Body: Race, Reproduction, and the Meaning of Liberty*. New York: Vintage.

Roberts, D. (2016). *Fatal Invention: How Science, Politics, and Big Business Re-create Race in the Twenty-First Century*. New York: The New Press.

2
Locked spaces, locked voice Language, muteness, and institutional control

In the UK, psychiatric institutions continue to function as extensions of broader systems of racialised and gendered control. Their apparent neutrality – expressed through white coats, clinical routines, and laminated rights leaflets – masks the deep asymmetries of power they reproduce. For Black women, these are not just spaces of care, but sites of epistemic violence, carceral containment, and institutional mistrust too.

Drawing from interviews with Black women detained under the Mental Health Act in various parts of the country, this chapter foregrounds the shared structural conditions that govern our institutional experiences. These accounts are not offered as isolated cases, but as evidence of systemic practice. The narratives reveal a consistent pattern of diagnostic overreach, silencing, misinterpretation, and bureaucratic erasure.

The work of Ahmed (2012) and Bhopal (2018) is instructive here. Both authors foreground the institutional mechanisms by which complaints, refusals, and alternative readings are rendered unintelligible or punished. Psychiatric wards – like many other public institutions – operate through what Ahmed calls the "institutional mechanics of being heard": who is believed, whose pain is legible, and whose voice carries consequence. In this sense, the ward is not a deviation from institutional norm, but a concentrated expression of it.

As Foucault (1977) reminds us, institutions derive their power not only from confinement but from their capacity to categorise and codify. Within this framework, Black women are often read through a matrix of suspicion as hostile, as unstable, as deceptive. Hartman (1997) calls these misreadings "scenes of subjection" – moments in which Black women are made hyper-visible to institutional scrutiny yet invisible as speaking subjects.

One woman from a London unit recalled: "I kept asking to see the psychiatrist. They kept telling me I already had. I hadn't. I realised my voice didn't matter – only my file did." This statement exemplifies what Fricker (2007) terms epistemic injustice: the denial of someone's credibility as a knower of their own experience. Here, the institutional record (the file) is granted more authority than the patient's own memory and voice. This reflects a systemic logic where Black women are made invisible as subjects and hyper-visible as risk categories.

Moreover, this incident reveals a form of bureaucratic violence (Fassin, 2012), where harm is enacted not through overt aggression but through administrative indifference. The file, once completed, functions as a truth-making device: it documents encounters that never occurred, erases those that did, and reorders the patient's reality to fit institutional expectations.

It also resonates with Ahmed's (2012) critique of institutional mechanisms that pre-empt dissent by rendering certain voices illegible. In this context, the patient's effort to advocate for herself is not only dismissed but also rewritten. Her presence is overridden by documentation and her agency reduced to a clerical error.

Finally, the quote underscores the paradox of surveillance and disregard. Black women in psychiatric care are closely watched but not truly seen. They are monitored for compliance, yet their needs and narratives are systematically excluded from the frameworks that determine care.

These testimonies are not anomalies. They form a body of evidence. This chapter centres these composite narratives to examine how institutional silencing is produced not just through omission but through a calculated narrowing of interpretive possibility. Black women are not only misread but made unreadable by the systems that claim to monitor our well-being.

I trace how this process unfolds: through routine sedation, the language used in files, assumptions made by staff, and disciplinary spatiality. As Crenshaw (1989) and Bowleg (2021) argue, intersectionality must remain a tool for structural analysis, which is not only a tool for description of identity but also a framework for understanding institutional harm.

This is not simply a chapter about women who were detained. It is a chapter about who is deemed detainable, who is listened to, and who is systematically silenced when the doors close.

The architecture of compliance

Once inside the ward, daily routines take on a disciplinary rhythm. Wake times, mealtimes, medication rounds, and scheduled "activities" are not about therapeutic engagement but about establishing control. The structure is rigid by design – every moment accounted for, every deviation pathologised. This is what Foucault (1977) terms the "microphysics of power," a system in which docility is produced by routine rather than force.

Several women described how surveillance extended beyond cameras to staff interactions. One participant from a unit in Birmingham reflected: "If I sat alone, I was seen as withdrawn. If I asked too many questions, I was agitated. You couldn't win. There was only one right way to be – and it wasn't being like me." Here, the ward operates as what Goffman (1961) calls a "total institution" – a closed system that strips individuals of their identity and replaces it with institutional logic. For Black women, this logic is further filtered through the lenses of race and gender. As Gilmore (2007) and Davis (2003) argue in carceral scholarship, the state does not just detain bodies, it disciplines them so that they form eligible categories of threat or compliance.

Silence becomes a condition of temporary safety. Women spoke about withholding emotion, suppressing frustration, and even modulating their tone of voice to avoid being labelled disruptive. Yet these acts of restraint were also used against them. One woman said: "I stayed quiet because I was scared. Later, they said I was emotionally flat and detached. Even my silence was seen as pathology." In these moments, diagnostic frameworks collapse into racialised surveillance. Staff notes become tools of interpretation that often misread restraint as illness or coded language as defiance. The institution trains patients to be compliant and then uses that compliance as evidence of disorder.

This disciplinary structure is masked by a veneer of medical neutrality. As Metzl (2009) argues in *The Protest Psychosis*, psychiatric institutions often racialise diagnostic categories while presenting them as objective science. For Black women, this means that acts of self-protection – withdrawal, silence, questioning authority – are read not as contextually rational but as symptoms of pathology.

The file becomes a carceral script, shaping the narrative of the patient's identity and trajectory. Gumbs (2020) reminds us that paperwork within carceral logic functions not merely as record-keeping but as a kind of narrative incarceration fixing people in place as unstable, disobedient, or irrational. This reinforces what Browne (2015) identifies as the afterlife of surveillance, a system wherein Black bodies are continuously scrutinised, regulated, and misread through logic inherited from slavery and colonial discipline.

Even in silence, the Black woman's body is not free from interpretation as it becomes a site of projection and speculation. Her resistance, even when quiet, is rendered illegible. Her fear is read as detachment. Her difference becomes deviance. As Collins (2000) and Lorde (1984) have long asserted, Black women's embodied knowledge is rarely granted legitimacy within white institutional frameworks. In psychiatric care, this illegibility becomes a mode of containment.

To be read wrongly is not only to be misunderstood, but it is to be disciplined accordingly too. The institution does not simply erase identity. It rewrites it. And then files it away.

Sedation as silencing: Pharmaceutical compliance and erasure

One of the most frequently cited tools of control in the psychiatric ward is medication. For the women in this study, sedation was rarely described as therapeutic – it was understood as a form of silencing. A participant from Manchester said,"They didn't want to talk to you,they just wanted you quiet."

Sedation functions as both a pharmacological and a political mechanism. As Martin-Baró (1994) warns in his analysis of psychiatry under authoritarian regimes, psychiatric drugs can become tools of pacification rather than of care – dulling not only pain, but protest. In the UK context, overmedication has become a practice of institutional management: a way to suppress rather than understand.

Participants reported feeling chemically subdued wondering why this was deemed necessary. Consent was often assumed, not obtained. As one woman recalled: "I wasn't refusing to take my meds. I just asked what they were. That alone made them suspicious. After that, they started injecting me without warning." This echoes the concerns of disability justice theorists such as Piepzna-Samarasinha (2018), who argue that compliance-based models of care strip disabled people, especially those of colour of agency. Medication is deployed not to relieve suffering but to restore institutional order. Refusing or questioning treatment is read as non-compliance, not self-advocacy.

Moreover, sedation has consequences beyond the moment. Many described memory gaps, dissociation, and an altered sense of time. The ward, already stripped of sensory texture, becomes even less navigable under heavy medication. "You forget what day it is," said one participant."And then they write that down too as more evidence that you're not well."

Here, we see how biomedical authority colludes with institutional documentation to overwrite embodied narratives. The medicated patient is often presumed truthful only when compliant, while any trace of resistance is pathologised as instability a dynamic that resonates with Foucault's (1977) analysis of "docile bodies" and with Williams, Martin and Gabe's (2011) account of pharmaceuticalisation as a mode of governance.In this framework, sedation becomes more than a treatment: it is a disciplinary act, and neutralises dissent, flattens complexity, and ensures that the institution remains unchallenged. For Black women in particular, whose emotions are already read through a racialised lens: sedation is not about healing, it is about removal. A removal from space, from speech, from self.

This logic of removal mirrors what Mbembe (2003) terms "necropolitics" on the use of social and institutional structures to determine whose lives are rendered grievable, whose suffering is worth responding to, and whose existence can be reduced to functionality. Psychiatric sedation in this context becomes a means of erasing discomfort both for the patients and the staff without addressing its origins.

A participant from a South London ward remarked: "I felt like I was being disappeared. I was there, but only my body. My thoughts, my fear, my story – —none of that mattered." Such testimony challenges the assumption that medical care is inherently benevolent. As Sweeney (2016) notes, psychiatry in the UK has often functioned through coercive paradigms where Black patients are disproportionately medicated, restrained, and pathologised. This is compounded by the historical mistrust between racialised communities and state care systems (Fernando, 2010).

Moreover, when sedation becomes the primary response to emotional distress, it flattens the social causes of that distress into individual dysfunction. It absolves the institution of having to ask what led to the patient's condition in the first place. In doing so, it reasserts the idea that Black women must be corrected, not supported that their healing must be controlled rather than enabled.

In these ways, sedation functions not as an interruption of institutional violence, but as its silent continuation.

This also aligns with Metzl and Roberts's (2014) call to interrogate what they term the "racial bioethics" of psychiatric care: how policies and clinical norms often fail to account for the racialised body as a site of historical and structural vulnerability. When institutional responses to distress are reduced to pharmacological restraint, they reinforce a form of care that pathologises grief, anger, and protest as symptoms rather than signals.

Some women reported that being sedated also carried reputational consequences inside the ward. "They'd say I was 'on the radar' now," one participant shared, "as if once you're medicated, you're no longer trustworthy." This stigma added an internal layer of control, where medication not only silenced but also marked. Women began to police their behaviour to avoid escalation; these kinds of strategies are rooted in fear rather than recovery.

The cumulative effect of this is a kind of institutional forgetting. Sedation erases memory, dulls presence, and fragments continuity. As Jackson (2020) notes, when memory is disrupted by trauma and medication, it becomes harder to narrate your experience, to make claims, or to seek redress. In this way, sedation serves both an immediate disciplinary function and a long-term epistemic one: it removes the capacity for testimony.

What emerges is a psychiatric landscape in which medication operates as a form of narrative foreclosure. It precludes not only certain behaviours but the right to explain them. For Black women already made illegible through race and gender, this compounds a deeper dispossession – the erasure not only of their voices, but of memories, motives, and meanings.

Beyond medication and surveillance, another mechanism through which Black women are silenced in psychiatric institutions is documentation – how things are written down, interpreted, and filed. The file becomes a living artefact of institutional truth, and what is recorded carries more authority than what is said. This is what Gumbs (2020) refers to as "narrative incarceration," where clinical notes, incident reports, and behavioural summaries construct a version of the self that may bear little resemblance to lived experience.

> Several women in our interviews reported inaccuracies in their records – conversations that never occurred, behaviours they never exhibited, refusals they never made. Yet, once these are written down, they are treated as facts. A participant from Leeds recounted:They wrote that I was being aggressive because I stood up during ward round. I wasn't shouting or anything. I just stood up. But from then on, every interaction was filtered through that note.

The transformation of ordinary actions into evidence of pathology reflects what Benjamin (2019) calls the "coded inequities" of institutional systems: the ways in which Black individuals are disproportionately flagged, indexed, and escalated through algorithmic or bureaucratic processes. While Benjamin develops this concept in relation to digital technologies, the same logic applies in psychiatric settings where institutional practices are designed to amplify perceived risk rather than interpret behaviours in their social or cultural context. Hartman's (1997) concept of "scenes of subjection" resurfaces here not just in physical control but in representational capture. The written record becomes a performance of authority: it determines how the patient is treated, what responses are considered appropriate, and how decisions about medication or restraint are justified. This kind of administrative authorship becomes a form of power that cannot be contested from within.

Women described the futility of trying to correct their records. "It's your word against theirs," one participant said. "But their version has a badge and a clipboard." The institutional preference for staff narratives over patient testimony reflects a deeper epistemic hierarchy – what Spivak (1988) identifies as the inability of the subaltern to speak. Even when Black women do speak in the context of psychiatric care, they are routinely misheard, misread, or strategically ignored.

This process is not incidental – it is structural. It creates a feedback loop where documentation leads to greater control, greater control leads to more documentation, and the patient becomes increasingly trapped in an institutional narrative that rewrites resistance as disorder.

Mills (1997) reminds us in his work on the epistemology of ignorance, that systems of knowledge are never neutral – they are designed to preserve certain power relations. In psychiatric institutions, the knowledge produced about patients often centres whiteness, male authority, and clinical detachment. The perspectives of racialised women are not only absent; they are actively disqualified. This becomes a form of administrative violence: harm is enacted through the symbolic authority of paper, file, and digital trace rather than through physical force.

Some participants said that even after discharge, their records continued to shape how future professionals treated them. "My GP looked at my history and started acting weirdly cautious," one woman said. "I was being pre-judged by something someone else wrote about me months ago."

Thus the labelling machine has consequences that outlast the institutional stay. It inscribes a legacy of distrust that travels across services, shaping every subsequent interaction. It also complicates efforts to seek justice or appeal decisions, since the documentation itself is framed as neutral evidence rather than subjective interpretation.

In such spaces, truth is not what happened. Truth is what gets recorded. And for Black women that truth is often a distortion that justifies further containment, exclusion, and disbelief both inside and beyond the ward.

Discharge without liberation: Surveillance after care

For many Black women, discharge from the ward does not equate to freedom – it marks the beginning of another chapter of scrutiny. While the physical confinement ends, the institutional gaze follows. Follow-up care is often framed not in terms of healing or community integration but in terms of risk management and compliance monitoring.

Participants spoke of feeling as though they had been placed on a permanent watch list. "I still have to meet a community nurse weekly," one woman explained. "She acts more like a parole officer than a support worker." This surveillance-oriented approach reinforces the idea that Black women's recovery is never complete and that they remain suspect, their every move a potential trigger for reintervention.

Fanon's (1967) insights on colonial psychiatry remain hauntingly relevant here. He describes how the colonised subject is never truly rehabilitated in the eyes of the coloniser; they are always one incident away from relapse, from reclassification, from being returned to the institution. Psychiatric aftercare for Black women reproduces this logic: the idea that their minds and by extension their bodies are inherently unstable.

The burden of demonstrating "wellness" falls disproportionately on the discharged patient. They must perform normality and over-perform compliance. Any sign of distress – fatigue, sadness, or disagreement – can be reread as regression. As Crenshaw (1991) reminds us, intersectionality is not only about multiple forms of oppression but also about the intensified scrutiny that results from occupying those intersections.

One of the most difficult aspects participants shared was the virtual impossibility of choosing not to take medication. Once medication was prescribed, any questioning of the medication plan – even mild hesitation – was read as either a lack of insight or a sign of deterioration. "You can't just say you're tired or sad like everyone else," a participant from Birmingham explained. "If you do, they say you need more meds. It's like being trapped in a cycle where your humanity is the symptom."

This pattern reflects what Metzl (2009) calls the "pharmaceuticalization of Black distress," where medication becomes the primary response to social suffering and structural causes such as racism, isolation, or poverty are ignored. Rather than engaging in meaningful dialogue about context or trauma, clinicians often double down on pharmacological management. The medicalised framing of Black emotion limits the space for ordinary human variation. Sadness, anger, or confusion are not viewed as valid responses to complex life experiences, but treated as chemical imbalances to be fixed.

This expanded form of surveillance often intersects with social services, education, and employment, where psychiatric labels are quietly passed along in paperwork, shaping opportunities, benefits, and mobility. For Black women, this translates into being doubly excluded: first by the ward and then by the world that believes the ward's version of them.

Thus, institutionalisation is not a bounded event but a protracted condition. Its afterlife is managed through subtle forms of control that masquerade as care. Discharge becomes a misnomer – what is released is not the person, but their file into the bloodstream of institutional networks that continue to decide where and how they belong.

Conclusion

Locked spaces do not end when the doors open. What this chapter has shown is that the psychiatric ward functions not as a site of healing but as a node in a larger web of institutional control. For Black women, entry into these spaces is often involuntary; their care is framed through suspicion, their speech is filtered through bureaucratic mechanisms, and their resistance is rendered pathological.

We have seen how documentation and labelling function as tools of administrative violence, how medication is prescribed as a proxy for containment, and how discharge is less a release and more a continuation of surveillance. Institutional power does not need bars and handcuffs – it only needs procedures, notes, and assumptions.

The voices shared in this chapter confirm that what is recorded often bears little resemblance to what is lived. And yet these records shape the future. They determine access to services, credibility with professionals, and perceptions within the community. In this way, the ward is not a singular event but a durable structure whose architecture persists long after the patient has left.

The challenge, then, is not simply to critique the institution but to unsettle the truths it claims to produce. To name the violence in its silences. And to reclaim the voices it sought to erase.

Reflexive questions

1. How does institutional documentation shape the identities and futures of racialised women within and beyond psychiatric settings?
2. In what ways does psychiatric medication function as a disciplinary mechanism rather than a therapeutic tool?

3. What assumptions underpin the continued surveillance of Black women after discharge?
4. How can we challenge the authority of clinical records when they contradict lived experience?
5. What would a truly liberatory model of mental health care for Black women look like?

References

Ahmed, S. (2012). *On Being Included: Racism and Diversity in Institutional Life*. Durham, Duke University Press.

Benjamin, R. (2019). *Race After Technology: Abolitionist Tools for the New Jim Code*. Cambridge: Polity Press.

Bhopal, K. (2018). *White privilege: The myth of a post-racial society*. Bristol: Policy Press.

Bowleg, L. (2021). 'Evolving intersectionality within public health: From analysis to action', *American Journal of Public Health*, 111(1), pp. 88–90.

Browne, S. (2015). *Dark matters: On the surveillance of Blackness*. Durham: Duke University Press.

Collins, P. H. (2000). *Black feminist thought: Knowledge, consciousness, and the politics of empowerment*. 2nd edn. New York: Routledge.

Crenshaw, K. (1989). 'Demarginalizing the intersection of race and sex: A Black feminist critique of antidiscrimination doctrine, feminist theory and antiracist politics', *University of Chicago Legal Forum*, 1989(1), pp. 139–167.

Crenshaw, K. (1991). Mapping the margins: Intersectionality, identity politics, and violence against women of color. *Stanford Law Review*, 43(6), 1241–1299.

Davies, C. B. (2003). *Black women, writing and identity: Migrations of the subject*. 2nd edn. London: Routledge.

Fanon, F. (1967). *Black skin, white masks*. Translated by C. L. Markmann. New York: Grove Press.

Fassin, D. (2012). *Humanitarian reason: A moral history of the present*. Translated by R. Gomme. Berkeley: University of California Press.

Fernando, S. (2010). *Mental health, race and culture*. 3rd edn. Basingstoke: Palgrave Macmillan.

Foucault, M. (1977). *Discipline and punish: The birth of the prison*. Translated by A. Sheridan. New York: Pantheon Books.

Fricker, M. (2007). *Epistemic injustice: Power and the ethics of knowing*. Oxford: Oxford University Press.

Gilmore, R. W. (2007). *Golden Gulag: Prisons, surplus, crisis, and opposition in globalizing California*. Berkeley: University of California Press.

Goffman, E. (1961). *Asylums: Essays on the social situation of mental patients and other inmates*. New York: Anchor Books.

Gumbs, A. P. (2020). *Dub: Finding Ceremony*. Durham, NC: Duke University Press.

Hartman, S. (1997). *Scenes of Subjection: Terror, Slavery, and Self-Making in Nineteenth-Century America*. Oxford: Oxford University Press.

Jackson, Z. I. (2020). *Becoming human: Matter and meaning in an antiblack world*. New York: New York University Press.

Lorde, A. (1984). *Sister outsider: Essays and speeches*. Freedom, CA: Crossing Press.

Martín-Baró, I. (1994). *Writings for a liberation psychology*. Edited by A. Aron and S. Corne. Cambridge, MA: Harvard University Press.

Mbembe, A. (2003). 'Necropolitics', *Public Culture*, 15(1), pp. 11–40.

Metzl, J. M. (2009). *The protest psychosis: How schizophrenia became a Black disease*. Boston: Beacon Press.

Metzl, J. M. and Roberts, D. E. (2014). 'Structural competency meets structural racism: Race, politics, and the structure of medical knowledge', *AMA Journal of Ethics*, 16(9), pp. 674–690.

Mills, C. W. (1997). *The Racial Contract*. Ithaca, NY: Cornell University Press.

Piepzna-Samarasinha, L. L. (2018). *Care work: Dreaming disability justice*. Vancouver: Arsenal Pulp Press.

Spivak, G. C. (1988). 'Can the subaltern speak?', in Nelson, C. and Grossberg, L. (eds.) *Marxism and the interpretation of culture*. Urbana, IL: University of Illinois Press, pp. 271–313.

Sweeney, A., Clement, S., Filson, B. and Kennedy, A. (2016). 'Trauma-informed mental healthcare in the UK: what is it and how can we further its development?', *Mental Health Review Journal*, 21(3), pp. 174–192.

Williams, S. J., Martin, P. and Gabe, J. (2011). 'The pharmaceuticalisation of society? A framework for analysis', *Sociology of Health & Illness*, 33(5), pp. 710–725.

3

Violence in uniforms Coercion by staff, security, and police in psychiatric institutions

The violence of the uniform began before I even entered the ward. It started at my doorstep with the knock I will never forget, the flashing lights, and the strangers in green who called my name like it didn't belong to me. There is something distinctly performative about the way uniforms operate in the UK. They do not just signal a professional role; they also signal legitimacy, authority, and permission. To wear a uniform is to be granted access to spaces, to decisions, and to power over another person's life.

In this chapter, I explore how uniforms function as technologies of power anchored in colonial histories, racial capitalism, and the medical-industrial complex. Drawing on Hartman's (1997) insights into subjection, Crenshaw's (1989) intersectionality, and Ahmed (2012) institutional critique, I weave personal memory with participant testimony to understand how institutional violence is enacted through everyday performances of care. Uniforms are not neutral; they mask harm, codify authority, and structure complicity.

My reflections are not singular; they are situated in a broader pattern of control and symbolic power that targets Black bodies, particularly those of women. In the UK's psychiatric system, uniformed power shows up in banal ways: the calm insistence on medication, the clipped refusal to answer questions, the silence in response to pain. These moments do not scream; they accumulate. And they do so under the legitimacy conferred by lanyards, scrubs, and badges.

The uniform, I argue, is a silent accomplice in these systems of domination. It grants cover to violence and distance to those who wear it. It tells the public "trust me." And too often, it tells the patient "you have no power here."

That power did not always wear blue or green scrubs in the ward. Sometimes, it wore a badge, a lanyard, or a clipped tone that made cruelty sound like care. Violence, when it came, arrived in raised voices or physical restraint, but it often came in the calm delivery of medication that had not been requested, in the casual denial of fresh air, or in the decision to withhold a phone call. And disturbingly often, it came from staff who looked like us.

This chapter confronts one of the most unsettling realities reported by participants: that harm inside institutions often wears the face of those who we least expect it from. When I was in the ward, it was not always the white staff who inflicted the most hurt. I remember one healthcare assistant – Black, like me – who refused to speak to me as if I was anything but a number.

She called out my surname as if I was a file to be retrieved. When I asked gently for a blanket, she waved her hand at me dismissively and didn't bring me one. When I sat alone in distress, she looked past me. These moments cut differently. They echo the quiet betrayals that institutions rely on to keep functioning without direct confrontation – what Crenshaw (1989) might describe as the intersection of race, gender, and institutional policy colliding to obscure accountability, or what Collins (2000) refers to as the controlling images that shape how Black women are expected to behave. In this case, the betrayal is structural rather than simply interpersonal. The silence, dismissal, and neglect I experienced were not isolated incidents, but embedded in an institutional logic that positions emotional withdrawal as professionalism and detachment as care.

Reading through my notes, I saw a pattern: the same assistant who enforced silence on my ward was also praised by her colleagues as "efficient." What does it mean to survive in a place like that by aligning with power? What does it do to the soul of someone whose own history might not be so far removed from mine?

Participants voiced the same confusion and pain. As I listened to the interviews again, the word that kept returning was "shocked"; shocked that someone from a similar background could act with such coldness, and yet also an awareness that institutional power rewards such detachment. This is not a matter of individual betrayal; it is an institutional strategy. As Hartman (1997) reminds us, subjection is most effective when enacted by those who themselves occupy the margins. When marginalised people are conscripted into enforcing institutional power, the lines between victim and enforcer blur. This chapter interrogates those tensions and the moral confusion they produce by weaving my experience with those of others who were detained, sedated, and silenced under the guise of medical care. It contributes a framework for understanding institutional complicity through the lens of racialised performance, drawing on intersectionality (Crenshaw, 1989), institutional affect (Ahmed, 2012), and subjection (Hartman, 1997) to examine how uniforms and authority structures produce compliance, alienation, and internalised surveillance within psychiatric care.

Uniforms as instruments of control

Uniforms operate as a visual shorthand for authority. They carry the weight of institutional credibility and often go unquestioned in terms of their ability to override personal agency. The act of uniforming someone, whether through scrubs, a lanyard, or a name badge, reinscribes a hierarchy that separates the caregiver from the patient and the enforcer from the subject. In psychiatric contexts, this uniformity is often conflated with safety. A calm tone, a pressed shirt, a badge of access: all are signs that signal trustworthiness, regardless of the actual practice of care.

Uniforms carry colonial legacies. As Fanon (1967) wrote, the coloniser wears his power, and it is recognised before a word is spoken. In contemporary UK institutions, that history continues in the form of procedural dominance and bureaucratic certainty. Power arrives not as compassion, but as protocol. Resistance is interpreted not as trauma but as disorder.

The illusion of institutional accountability is further reinforced by government responses that deny systemic fault. In response to a complaint submitted by one participant to the Home Office regarding police conduct, a letter dated 25 June 2025 was received, stating: "There is no evidence to suggest that officers acted outside the bounds of professional behaviour." This generic, dismissive response typifies a broader institutional deflection strategy – by framing the incident as isolated and professionally handled, the system evades engagement with the structural conditions that produce such harm. As Foucault might suggest, this is not merely bureaucratic negligence, but a mechanism of state power that transforms structural violence into a matter of individual oversight. Rather than acknowledging patterns of racialised harm, the state relies on abstract neutrality and procedural closure. Such language mirrors what patients in psychiatric care frequently encounter: violence rendered invisible by the professional tone of those delivering it and accountability buried beneath technical phrasing and institutional inertia.

Violation is not always physical. Many participants described emotional and spiritual violations that occurred under the guise of care. One participant recalled being taken in the middle of a family meal – no time for goodbyes and no explanation offered. Others spoke about having their prayers interrupted, being denied access to pastors, imams, or elders. One woman said, "They came while I was eating with my mum. I didn't even get to finish. Just taken, like I was a risk for sitting down." The cruelty of these removals lies not only in the act itself but in the calculated severance from ordinary human connection.

Participants noted that families often felt powerless to intervene because they were overwhelmed, unfamiliar with mental health systems, or fearful of making things worse. As Goffman

(1961) observes in his seminal work on total institutions, depersonalisation is a technique of control. In psychiatric spaces, this often takes the form of denying the patient's relational identity – their roles as daughter, parent, neighbour – and reducing them instead to a diagnosis or risk assessment.

In my case, the refusal of the institution to accept accountability for its actions was compounded by the behaviour of the officers themselves. When I insisted on sitting down rather than being manhandled, one of the police officers grabbed my breast under the guise of restraint. The pain was sharp, violating. My reaction – to bite – was framed not as self-defence but as assault. I was left surrounded by four large white officers for hours, waiting for an assessment that came late at night. My protest, my refusal to accept their handling of me, was pathologised. And what followed – my transport by ambulance, the handling by hospital porters, the disdain from staff in every uniformed role – was a continuation of the same logic: you are not a person, you are a problem. Even the porter who wheeled me into the ward acted with rudeness and disdain. My husband later told me he challenged the porter because he was shocked by how he was treating me and speaking to me as if I was beneath him.

These experiences make it clear that the issue is not limited to medical staff or police. It includes porters, security guards, and cleaners; every uniformed layer of the institution is infused with an ideology that permits dehumanisation. Each actor in the chain, however low paid or marginalised themselves, performs a role in upholding the illusion of order. This is why the violence of the uniform is so difficult to challenge: it is systemic, dispersed, and protected by a network of bureaucratic shielding.

Participant testimonies echo this diffusion of violence. One recalled, "The porter pushed the chair like I was cargo. No eye contact, no words. Just moved me like I wasn't there." Another described how "the cleaner stepped over my legs with the mop, looked at me, and kept moving." These everyday microaggressions are not incidental; they are a form of institutional communication. They comprise a performance of detachment that is designed to remind the patient of their place in the hierarchy.

This complicity also extended to low-paid staff such as cleaners and caterers, many of whom were migrants or racialised minorities themselves. Participants recounted incidents when these workers displayed disdain, mockery, or indifference towards patients, aligning themselves with institutional authority. Whether through small acts of cruelty or the deliberate ignoring of distress, these staff enacted a form of classed and racialised complicity that reflects broader hierarchies. As with care assistants, their proximity to suffering did not always translate into empathy. Rather, the institution often rewarded detachment and assimilation to dominant norms. These workers, many themselves precariously employed and surveilled, performed loyalty to the institution through silence, avoidance, or subtle policing. This reminds us that complicity is not just top-down; it is diffused throughout the institution and reinforced by class, migration status, and the internalisation of institutional norms.

As Fanon (1961) notes in *The Wretched of the Earth*, colonial orders sustain themselves by enlisting the oppressed in the management of their own. Here, the postcolonial institution repeats the logic: cleaners, porters, and other low-paid workers – often Black or Brown – become agents of containment, their uniforms offering a symbolic distance from those they are tasked with disciplining. We might think of this not only as racialised complicity but as a form of disciplinary assimilation where institutional survival requires silence as well as performance of loyalty to the dominant order.

We can build from this a new analytic: diversity as discipline. This concept captures how institutions mobilise inclusion not to transform structures but to enforce them. Uniforms and badges are tools of this disciplining: they enable low-paid racialised workers to be both vulnerable and powerful, subject to control, yet enforcers of it. This duality is not accidental; it is systemic and is designed to ensure the institution's continuity with minimal resistance.

In the next section, we turn to the symbolic performance of care through lanyards and diversity branding and the growing distance between institutional messaging and lived experience.

Badges, branding, and the illusion of inclusion

As already noted, Badges and lanyards, too, are not innocent. The rainbow-striped lanyards that many NHS staff wear, symbolising a commitment to diversity and inclusion, sit in stark contrast to the racialised realities of psychiatric care. What does it mean to wear the colours of inclusion while enforcing exclusion? To carry the badge of care while participating in systems that silence, sedate, and surveil?

For many participants, the badge became a symbol of contradiction, of institutional branding over lived experience. One woman noted that her Bible was confiscated while a staff member with a "Faith and Inclusion" lanyard told her that it was for her own safety. Another was forced to break her fast under the supervision of a Black healthcare assistant who dismissed her religious observance as "delusion." One participant described being told, "Your ancestors are not here, only doctors are," after trying to explain her distress through a cultural lens. These moments reveal a deeper tension: symbols of diversity do not dismantle systems of coercion – they often mask them.

Uniformed staff routinely overlooked spiritual and cultural needs, categorising epistemologies such as ancestral communication, bewitchment, or divine presence as psychosis or non-compliance. These diagnostic framings assert Euro-Western psychiatric norms as the singular truth. Kleinman (1995) reminds us that medical systems are moral worlds that are grounded in normative assumptions. Further, Collins (2000) argues that institutional inclusion often requires submission to dominant ideologies, making difference visible only when it conforms to accepted norms.

Badges, then, do not simply signify care; they legitimise surveillance. A staff member wearing a "Diversity Champion" badge dismissed a patient's prayer ritual as "magical thinking." A porter wearing a rainbow NHS sticker refused to make eye contact when a patient cried out for water. Such an accessory becomes what Ahmed (2012) calls a "mechanism for avoiding doing anything" – what we might extend here to mean a form of diversity as discipline. This concept captures how inclusion is weaponised as optics to manage dissent, flatten cultural variance, and suppress critique. The lanyard becomes a progressive alibi, its colours a camouflage.

Even low-paid, often migrant, workers – such as cleaners, porters, and caterers – are folded into this architecture of symbolic and material control. Though not always fluent in English or fully integrated into institutional culture, these workers learn quickly how to participate in its hierarchies. As one participant shared, "The cleaner never looked me in the eye. She walked past my cries like I was furniture." Another recounted a moment when a porter barked at her to move faster, even though she was sedated and dizzy: "He had a little NHS badge on and told me, 'We're all just doing our job.' But his job didn't include seeing me as human."

This enactment of control by those who are themselves structurally marginalised reflects what Moten and Harney (2013) describe in *The Undercommons* of how institutions co-opt precarious workers into the reproduction of power. These workers, many of them racialised immigrants, are both surveilled and enforcers of surveillance. Their lanyards, uniforms, and minor authority offer a sense of legitimacy and protection, what Fanon (1967) calls "the prestige of the uniform" in colonial regimes. The effect is a hollowing out of empathy, which is replaced by bureaucratic alignment.

Moreover, these dynamics continue a longer genealogy. As Metzl (2010) and Fernando (2017) argue, psychiatry has long pathologised non-Western expressions of emotion, protest, and grief. When combined with hierarchical workplace structures, even those closest to patients – by proximity or shared racial identity – are drawn into the logic of discipline. One participant said, "The porter was African like me. But he wouldn't even say hello. He treated me like I'd done something wrong." This betrayal stings differently; it echoes what Hartman (1997) and Gilroy (2005) remind us of: that the violence of the institution is often more effective when enacted by the familiar.

Wearing the badge, even by those racialised as Black or Brown, does not ensure empathy. Rather, the badge often functions as a tool of erasure. It signals professional identity but obscures the humanity beneath. Participants described being labelled "non-compliant" or "paranoid" when referencing dreams, visitations, or spiritual callings. "I said my grandmother visited me in a dream to give me peace. They increased my dose," recalled one woman. This echoes Goffman's (1961) concept of depersonalisation of how institutions erase relational and cultural roles in favour of a flattened, medicalised identity.

As Fanon (1967) argues, colonial power is worn – it is performed through the uniform, the badge, and the scripted tone. And as Gilroy (2005) and Mbembe (2001) remind us, institutional power defines who is expendable and who is grievable. In psychiatric care, those seen as "diverse" are often rendered more surveilled and more silenced.

Even government institutions echo this deflection of responsibility. In response to questions about institutional failures and discrimination, the Home Office noted in a letter dated 25 June 2025: "Decisions taken by uniformed staff are operational matters for which no ministerial responsibility will be assumed unless policy failure is explicitly proven." This refusal to take ownership further entrenches the illusion of care, suggesting that uniforms grant impunity rather than responsibility. It mirrors the wider NHS environment where harm inflicted under the badge is disavowed as exceptional or individual rather than structural and repeated.

Wearing the badge, then, is not just about identity; it becomes a performative shield. Ahmed (2012) describes it as the "institutional smile" where it presents care while withholding accountability. In psychiatric contexts, these optics serve to shield institutions from critique while intensifying control over racialised, gendered, and spiritually diverse bodies.

In this framework, badges and lanyards are not signs of inclusion. They are artefacts of institutional discipline – tools that allow the system to co-opt care while maintaining control. They promise dignity but deliver silence. They promise care but facilitate harm.

We might therefore expand our analytic of diversity as discipline to read the badge as a cultural artefact of contemporary institutional governance where inclusion is aesthetic, not structural; performative, not reparative; and ultimately a tool to manage the very resistance it claims to embrace.

The gatekeepers of care: Class, migration, and the politics of proximity

Several participants noted the uneasy dynamics between patients and low-paid hospital workers, many of whom were racialised migrants. Rather than forming bonds of shared marginalisation, these staff were sometimes perceived as gatekeepers of institutional routine. Through silence, hurried dismissal, or mimicry of clinical authority, they contributed to the atmosphere of neglect. Their actions were not always overtly hostile, but they reinforced the patient-worker divide and echoed the unspoken hierarchies of race, class, and professional legitimacy that structured the ward environment. One participant described being removed from home while sleeping and taken to the hospital without explanation. Another said she was denied the chance to say goodbye to her children because the porter "was in a rush and wouldn't wait." These are not merely logistical failures; they are emotionally violent acts that strip people of their dignity and relational anchors. Such treatment echoes what Goffman (1961) observes in *Asylums*: that institutionalisation often begins with a symbolic death a severing from social roles and personal identity.

The badge or lanyard becomes the great equaliser here – not in liberatory terms, but in disciplinary ones. Even workers with limited English, minimal training, and precarious contracts quickly learned the authority the badge confers. "They think they're untouchable," one participant said of a hospital porter who shouted orders but ignored cries for help. These individuals, once marginalised themselves, become enforcers of the very system that invisibilises them.

Fanon (1967) warned us of this. In colonial systems, it was often the "native informant" or the low-ranking colonial soldier who administered the master's discipline. In the modern NHS, this figure may wear a cleaner's tunic, a porter's uniform, or a kitchen apron, but the function is the same: to police, to control, and to remind patients that care comes with conditions.

This is not to individualise blame, but to interrogate how institutional training, legal protections, and lack of oversight create a chain of impunity. The very workers who are often underpaid, overworked, and racialised become key instruments of discipline and exclusion. As Moten and Harney (2013) argue, the undercommons is not just a space of refusal, it is also a space where subjugation is negotiated. These workers exist within the institution's belly, close enough to power to replicate it but not far enough away to critique it without risking their own position.

Moral confusion and institutional betrayal

What makes these interactions especially devastating is the erosion of expected solidarities. Participants not only spoke of harm, they also spoke of betrayal. The betrayal came from within the margins: from fellow racialised people, from women of similar backgrounds, from those assumed to understand. One participant recalled, "It was a Brown woman who took my scarf off in front of male staff and laughed. That cut deep. I didn't expect that from her." Another described a Black care worker mocking her tears in patois, "like it was funny, like she was showing off in front of the nurses."

These are not isolated missteps but patterned breaches of relational trust, amplified by shared racial, cultural, or gendered reference points. Such betrayals deepen the trauma not just because of what is done but because of *who* does it. As bell hooks has written, betrayal within marginalised communities often hurts more profoundly than direct oppression, because it ruptures the hope of solidarity.

This dynamic reflects what we might term "relational inversion," which is when expected empathy becomes unexpected cruelty and presumed kinship is flipped into institutional allegiance. The system relies on such inversions. Hartman (1997) reminds us that domination is most effective when administered by those who themselves live under domination. The institution conscripts care workers, particularly racialised and gendered ones, into enforcer roles, granting them symbolic power through badges, lanyards, or keys. But this power is not emancipatory; it is disciplinary.

Fanon (1967) captures this moral ambivalence when he describes how the colonial soldier, though himself oppressed, became a vessel of the coloniser's will. In psychiatric wards, the betrayal lies not only in action but in affect: the cold tone, the denial of pain, the mocking laughter. These small acts of violence accumulate into moral injury.

We may understand this more broadly through the lens of the "instrumentalised resemblance," a term that captures how institutions weaponise perceived similarity to disarm resistance. A Black or Brown staff member rebuking a Black or Brown patient doesn't read as racialised harm to outsiders, but to the patient, it feels like abandonment. That is the genius of the system: it launders violence through proximity.

This moral confusion is systemic, not individual. It is produced through policies, reinforced by hierarchy, and protected by law. The institution thrives through betrayal rather than despite it – fracturing communities that might otherwise resist.

When combined with laws like Section 2 of the Mental Health Act, which permits detention without consent for up to 28 days on the grounds of mental disorder, the power these workers wield, however minimal on paper, becomes amplified. Section 2 strips individuals of agency, converting refusal into a symptom and protest into proof of illness. Once detained, the patient's legal personhood is suspended: their words lost evidentiary weight, their "no" becomes meaningless, and their pain can be disregarded in the name of care. This legal apparatus authorises not only doctors but entire networks of ward staff, porters, and even temporary agency workers to participate in the logic of containment. As Fernando (2017) argues, psychiatry in the UK remains structurally racist, enabling laws like Section 2 to disproportionately affect Black individuals and legitimise coercive treatment under the guise of clinical neutrality.

This transformation of vulnerability into docility reflects broader colonial inheritances. Fanon (1967) warns that the function of colonial law was never just to punish but also to remake the subject into one that complies with the ruling order. In the contemporary ward, Section 2 acts similarly: it does not just detain – it disciplines. It authorises those with even marginal institutional standing – cleaners, porters, auxiliary staff – to become actors in a carceral theatre of care. It produces what we might call *lateralised power*, where structural violence is enacted not just top-down but sideways too – delegated, distributed, and depersonalised.

Conclusion: The violence that smiles

Violence in institutions does not always arrive with force. Sometimes, it arrives as silence, as refusal, as indifference wrapped in lanyards and laced with policy language. Across testimonies and theories, we can see how harm is administered not just by systems but through the people they train, badge, and deputise.

From police to porters and from doctors to diversity officers, the theatre of care masks a machinery of control.

This chapter has shown that racialised and gendered violence in psychiatric settings is not incidental. It is structured, repeated, and sustained by aesthetic markers of professionalism and inclusion. Badges and uniforms offer both visibility and shield the actors who wear them. They facilitate complicity while muting dissent. And through laws like Section 2, the very right to refuse or to accept these forced and sometimes unnecessary treatments is erased.

To name this violence is not to indict individuals but to expose the ways in which institutions even make acts of cruelty look like care. Whether through the badge of a migrant cleaner or the clipped tone of a diversity-lanyard-wearing nurse, what emerges is a consistent grammar of erasure. And yet, the voices in this chapter also remind us that what is named can be resisted.

Reflective questions

1. How do symbols like badges and lanyards shape our perception of authority, care, and inclusion?
2. In what ways might low-paid staff be both victims of institutional violence and vehicles for its reproduction?
3. How does the use of Section 2 of the Mental Health Act illustrate the legal silencing of marginalised voices?
4. What does it mean for institutions to perform care while structurally enacting harm? How can we recognise and disrupt this performance?
5. How might recognising complicity across all levels of staff – from doctors to cleaners – shift our understanding of accountability and reform?

References

Ahmed, S. (2012). *On Being Included: Racism and Diversity in Institutional Life*. Duke University Press.

Collins, P. H. (2000). *Black Feminist Thought: Knowledge, Consciousness, and the Politics of Empowerment*. Routledge.

Fanon, F. (1961). *The wretched of the earth*. Translated by C. Farrington. New York: Grove Press.

Fanon, F. (1967). *Black skin, white masks*. Translated by C. L. Markmann. New York: Grove Press.

Fernando, S. (2017). *Institutional Racism in Psychiatry and Clinical Psychology: Race Matters in Mental Health*. Palgrave Macmillan.

Gilroy, P. (2005). *Postcolonial Melancholia*. Columbia University Press.

Goffman, E. (1961). *Asylums: Essays on the Social Situation of Mental Patients and Other Inmates*. Anchor Books.

Hartman, S. (1997). *Scenes of Subjection: Terror, Slavery, and Self-Making in Nineteenth-Century America*. Oxford University Press.

Kleinman, A. (1995). *Writing at the Margin: Discourse Between Anthropology and Medicine*. University of California Press.

Metzl, J. (2010). *The Protest Psychosis: How Schizophrenia Became a Black Disease*. Beacon Press.

Mbembe, A. (2001). *On the Postcolony*. University of California Press.

Moten, F. and Harney, S. (2013). *The Undercommons: Fugitive Planning and Black Study*. Minor Compositions.

4
The men in the room Patriarchy, power, and gendered violence in psychiatric care

Introduction

This chapter interrogates the gendered structures of violence within psychiatric institutions, paying particular attention to the role of men, especially African men, as enforcers of institutional power. While previous chapters have examined the racialised and carceral dimensions of psychiatric systems, here the analysis turns deliberately toward patriarchy as an operational logic. Drawing on Black feminist, postcolonial, and carceral studies, this chapter foregrounds how masculinity – when sanctioned by the institution – becomes both a method and a measure of psychiatric control.

The central claim is this: psychiatric institutions do not simply *include* men; they rely on them. Male authority is not incidental but instrumental, especially in contexts where race, migration, and institutional discipline intersect. Within such institutions, African men in particular are often employed to enact psychiatric authority through physical discipline, verbal dominance, and procedural coercion. Their actions are not reducible to individual pathology, nor are they culturally determined. Rather, they reflect a structurally produced performance of masculinity, rooted in colonial histories and maintained through institutional rewards.

This argument demands an analytic shift. Rather than viewing racialised male staff as victims of systemic racism alone, this chapter situates them as agents of patriarchal enforcement who perform a specific function in the psychiatric order. Drawing on the work of Fanon (1952), Oyěwùmí (1997), hooks (2004), and Wynter (2003), this chapter interrogates how colonial hierarchies of gender and race have shaped not only who is institutionalised but who is empowered to discipline. In psychiatric spaces, racialised men, particularly those from the African diasporas, are frequently positioned as both visible proof of "diverse" institutions and silent instruments of enforcement who carry out the most violent functions of care.

Crucially, this chapter does not pursue a narrative of betrayal or failed solidarity. It does not claim that racialised men have abandoned their communities. Instead, it explores how institutions of mental health construct and reward masculinised performances of control and how this disproportionately places Black and Brown women at the receiving end of layered violence that is racialised, gendered, and medicalised.

In doing so, this chapter makes two key contributions. First, it foregrounds patriarchy as a system of disciplinary power embedded in psychiatric infrastructure. Second, it challenges the assumption that a racialised presence within institutions necessarily equates to transformation. On the contrary, it argues that the psychiatric system is fully capable of incorporating racialised actors, particularly men, into its architecture, provided they reproduce its fundamental logic: control, silence, and punishment.

What follows is not a critique of men as individuals, but of masculinity as an institutional function. The psychiatric system does not need its enforcers to be white. It needs them to be obedient, authoritative, and willing to suppress resistance, especially when it comes from women. In many cases, African men have been positioned, trained, and valorised to do precisely that.

Within psychiatric institutions, authority is not only racialised but also profoundly gendered in its distribution and performance. Masculinity, in this context, functions as a technology of discipline – a set of behaviours, affective postures, and institutional permissions that converge in the male staff member who is not expected to care but to contain. This is particularly evident in the psychiatric context, where male staff, disproportionately racialised and often of African or Caribbean origin, are routinely deployed to carry out the institution's most visibly coercive tasks: forcing patients to take medication, restraining them, physically relocating them, and silencing them through verbal commands.

These roles are not assigned arbitrarily. Rather, they reflect the embedded logic that masculine authority is both effective and legitimate. When women resist medication, express emotional pain, or ask questions deemed disruptive, their actions are swiftly reinterpreted through psychiatric discourse as non-compliance or symptomology. Male staff are summoned not for therapeutic intervention but for their presumed capacity to enforce order through their physical presence by exercising control and by instilling fear.

As hooks (2004) observes, "Patriarchy has no gender." In this case, however, it has a function: to authorise male domination within systems ostensibly built for healing. Masculinity becomes the vehicle through which institutional power is exercised and reproduced, and male staff are both trained and expected to embody that power without hesitation. Their legitimacy rests not in care but in command of a situation.

The racial dynamics of this are particularly salient. The psychiatric system's capacity to incorporate African men as enforcers of discipline reflects a broader colonial logic in which racialised men, when permitted proximity to state power, are required to reproduce its violences. As Fanon (1952,) writes, "The colonized man will manifest this aggressiveness which has been deposited in his bones against his own people." Fanon's insight is crucial: when they are denied power under colonial rule and are later offered conditional authority within postcolonial institutions, some men come to internalise the very hierarchies they once resisted, enacting violence that is not in opposition to the system but is on its behalf.

This explanation is not intended to pathologise African men or frame their actions as individual moral failings. Rather, it illustrates how institutions of care often absorb and operationalise patriarchal power, particularly through racialised masculinities. Within such settings, African male staff may be positioned to enforce control or authority in ways that echo broader gendered violence, but are legitimised by the clinical environment. The harm is not simply personal; it is institutional, structured, and often enacted under the guise of professionalism. The African male staff member is often seen as both ideal and expendable – visible enough to perform institutional strength, invisible enough to escape scrutiny.

Masculinity in these settings is not simply one identity among many. It is a method, an operational strategy through which resistance is neutralised, bodies are subdued, and psychiatric legitimacy is maintained. The male figure becomes the mechanism of enforcement, particularly in relation to female patients whose expressions of agency or distress are interpreted as defiance.

Importantly, the assumption that this force is neutral – that it is mere "procedure" – relies on the institution's ability to render male power as naturalised, even therapeutic. But for those who experience it, there is no ambiguity. When a woman is pinned down, silenced, or injected against her will, the message is not that care is being delivered, but it is that she has been overruled by force. And in these moments, it is masculinity that speaks on behalf of the institution.

"He looked like me, but held me down"

The affective dissonance experienced when a person is subjected to physical violence by someone who appears culturally or racially familiar demands critical attention. Within psychiatric settings, where women of colour are disproportionately institutionalised and pathologised (Fernando, 2017), the violence enacted by African male staff is not merely interpersonal; but that it is emblematic of a wider structure of colonial, racialised patriarchy operating through state-sanctioned institutions.

In multiple encounters recounted by survivors, including the author's own experiences, African men were disproportionately involved in acts of direct coercion: restraining women during episodes of "non-compliance," administering forced injections, and executing verbal reprimands that bordered on humiliation. These acts were not exceptional; they were patterned. The men were summoned when resistance was visible. They arrived with the authority of the institution behind them and the expectation that they would subdue people.

There is a distinctive pain in witnessing this kind of violence executed by someone who, in another context, might be imagined as a protector or ally. It is not the sameness of skin tone or accent that is disturbing but the instrumentalisation of that sameness in the service of control. The man who holds a body down is doing so not as a community member but as an institutional figure, one whose authority is conferred through proximity to psychiatric legitimacy, not through cultural connection.

This enactment of control must be situated within the colonial genealogy of masculine authority as discipline. In colonial regimes, African men were frequently recruited into roles as wardens, guards, and enforcers of order over other colonised subjects. Fanon (1952) argues that this internalised violence becomes a distorted outlet for the aggression of the colonised male subject, who, once given sanctioned authority, projects discipline downward in order to approximate the power once withheld from him. Within the psychiatric institution, this pattern is reproduced through the normalisation of male-led control, where race does not obstruct patriarchal power but becomes a conduit for it.

Oyěwùmí (1997) offers a vital intervention here, arguing that colonialism imposed Western gender logics onto African societies, producing hierarchical binaries that previously held little relevance in many Indigenous cosmologies. As such, African masculinity, particularly in the diasporic and institutional contexts, must not be read as culturally static but as produced through colonial conditions, refracted through migration, and absorbed into the logic of institutional performance.

These men are not simply performing their duties. They are participating in what Wynter (2003) calls the production of "genre-specific humans" – those who are rendered legible to the state through their functionality. In this case, the "function" is the execution of psychiatric control. The violence enacted is not personal but structural, yet its execution is profoundly intimate.

When an African male staff member restrains a Black woman patient, the image carries with it centuries of imposed gender hierarchies, distorted relational dynamics, and the contemporary pressures of institutional survival. These acts of dominance are often not carried out reluctantly but with the precision and confidence of repetition. Some women recall the glee or satisfaction with which control was asserted, not necessarily as cruelty but as the performance of competence, masculinity, and professional legitimacy (hooks, 2004).

To name this violence is not to individualise blame. It is to recognise that psychiatric institutions have learned to outsource discipline to those whose identities render the system more palatable. A white institution administered through the bodies of Black and Brown men appears more diverse, more inclusive, and, paradoxically, less violent, even as it enacts the same logics of subjugation.

The men who held women down, insulted them, ignored their questions, and administered medications by force were not aberrations. They were fulfilling their roles in a gendered and racialised hierarchy of care. The fact that their violence was routinised, even banal, speaks not to their character but to the design of the institution itself.

Colonial patriarchy and the production of violent men

To understand the role of African men as enforcers within psychiatric institutions, one must locate their actions within the broader architecture of colonial patriarchy. Patriarchy, in this context, is not simply a system of male domination; it is a historically produced and institutionally maintained order that casts masculinity as control and femininity as disorder. The incorporation of African men into psychiatric roles of enforcement reflects a deep entanglement between colonial governance, institutional masculinity, and the racialised state.

As Oweyumi (1997) powerfully argues, Western colonial systems imposed rigid gender binaries and hierarchies on societies in

which gender had not previously functioned as a primary axis of social organisation. The very idea of masculinity as inherently authoritative, protective, and superior is not culturally Indigenous but colonially constructed. African male authority, especially in postcolonial institutional contexts, has thus been forged within the image of the colonial patriarch, a figure who gains legitimacy through proximity to Euro-Western notions of rationality, discipline, and state power.

Psychiatric institutions, with their emphasis on behavioural regulation and normative functioning, provide fertile ground for the reproduction of this patriarchal authority. In these settings, the ideal male staff member is not a healer but a manager of deviance. He is trained to interpret resistance as pathology, emotion as risk, and assertiveness as aggression, particularly when these emerge from women, especially from Black women. The African man, operating within this logic, is incentivised to perform a masculinity that aligns with institutional needs: it is distant, commanding, and physically assertive. One participant noted, "They never came to talk. If you said no, or asked too many questions, it was always the men they sent. Black men mostly. They didn't ask what was wrong. They came to restrain."

Fanon (1952) provides a foundational lens through which to view this dynamic. In *Black Skin, White Masks*, Fanon examines how the colonial subject internalises the logic of the coloniser, often redirecting his psychic trauma towards those he is permitted to control. The racialised man's desire for recognition within the systems of power frequently results in the reproduction of those very systems, which are then mediated through his own body. In psychiatric institutions, this aggressiveness becomes both sanctioned and routine.

However, this is not merely psychological. It is structural and material. In a context where Black and migrant men are marginalised in most professional sectors, the role of the psychiatric enforcer offers a rare site of authority. It is a position from which one is visible, respected, and insulated from the precarity that shapes so much of the migrant experience. The institutional performance of masculinity – through restraint, silence, and procedural control – thus becomes not just about power but about survival and legibility within the logics of the state. A second participant described it plainly: "Some of them liked being in charge. It was their job to make you small. I remember one saying, 'You people need to learn to listen.' He looked like me, but he acted like he owned me."

Wynter (2003) takes this further by arguing that modern institutions, including those relating to mental health, function through the production of genre-specific humans: individuals whose worth is defined by their capacity to perform institutionally sanctioned roles. In this schema, the African male psychiatric worker is not outside the colonial order – he is integral to it. His very legitimacy is conditioned on his willingness to suppress, to order, and to manage the very populations from which he may have emerged.

This contradiction is rarely acknowledged in institutional discourse. Diversity policies may celebrate the presence of African staff, but they rarely interrogate the function they are made to serve. That function is often gendered: men enforce, women

care. And when men care, particularly racialised men, their legitimacy is questioned. Yet when they dominate, their authority is confirmed.

In this sense, psychiatric institutions reproduce not only colonial racial hierarchies but also the colonial gender contract, in which male domination is read as professional competence and female refusal as deviance. The result is a structural alignment where African men are placed – sometimes willingly, sometimes under economic and social coercion – into roles that replicate the very systems of control from which they are historically estranged. Another participant captured this dynamic: "You could tell which ones felt powerful. It was like, 'If I'm not going to be respected out there, I will be respected in here.' That respect came at our expense."

Speaking about this does not individualise blame or demonise African men. It unmasks the institution's capacity to absorb racialised masculinity and redeploy it as instrumental force. It names how patriarchy is produced not just at the level of ideology but through training manuals, shift allocations, job expectations, and unspoken rules about who gets called when a woman resists.

Institutional masculinity and migrant aspiration

The institutional performance of masculinity among African men in psychiatric spaces must be understood within the broader context of migrant aspiration and structural precarity. Migration is not only a movement across borders, but a negotiation of worth, legibility, and survival. For many men of African descent, particularly those working in undervalued sectors of the public sphere, institutions such as the NHS offer one of the few avenues through which they may attain visibility, respect, and economic stability. Yet this visibility comes at a cost: their incorporation into institutional structures is conditional upon their willingness to perform dominance.

Masculinity in this setting becomes not just an identity but a currency – a performative mode of being that signals professional legitimacy, emotional restraint, and command over those deemed deviant or disorderly. These characteristics are not neutral; they are institutionally desired. Psychiatric systems in particular equate male authority with order and compliance, and racialised men are often positioned to perform this authority in ways that affirm the institution's internal logic.

As Connell (1995) theorises, masculinities are always hierarchically arranged, with hegemonic masculinity situated at the top – typically white, middle class, heterosexual, and emotionally restrained. However, subordinated or complicit masculinities may align with hegemonic forms to gain legitimacy. The African male psychiatric worker does not embody hegemonic masculinity in a white supremacist society, but he is permitted a proximate version of it, so long as he enacts it through control and containment. His authority is situational, temporary, and contingent on discipline.

This performative arrangement is not arbitrary. As Wilson (2012) observes in her work on migrant labour and care work, postcolonial subjects are often valued not for who they are but for how well they can reproduce state-sanctioned norms. In psychiatric spaces, African men are made legible through their reliability in managing dissent rather than through care. This management is gendered: the women they restrain, silence, and correct are not only patients but symbolic figures – figures who disrupt the narrative of order, who speak too loudly, who refuse medication, and who do not yield.

Participants in this study articulated these dynamics with painful clarity. Several noted that male staff, particularly those who had arrived through migrant healthcare recruitment pathways, seemed especially determined to assert their role as disciplinarians. One woman explained, "They were the ones who got respect. If they were strict, they got shifts. If they were soft, they got ignored." Another observed, "You could see it – being in charge made them feel seen. Like it meant something." These insights reveal the micro economy of power in which racialised men navigate visibility by adopting the state's posture: discipline, detachment, and control.

The appeal of institutional belonging is not difficult to understand. For many migrant men, the psychiatric ward is not merely a workplace, it is a space in which their masculinity is finally rendered useful, professional, and legitimate. Yet this legitimacy is premised on the reproduction of hierarchical violence. It is built through the subordination of others, most often women, and most often Black women whose voices, movements, and refusals disrupt the fragile order they are tasked with maintaining.

Gordon (1997), in *Her Majesty's Other Children*, writes that "the Black man may be authorised to police the racial order, but he is never exempt from it." This is the paradox: African men in psychiatric spaces may be asked to discipline others, but they are never free from the gaze that disciplines them. Their power is conditional. Their masculinity is weaponised but never fully trusted.

To identify this is not to undermine their humanity. It is to highlight the structural seduction of patriarchal alignment in institutions that reward suppression. Migrant aspiration, rooted in survival and shaped by exclusion, can be manipulated into a system of gendered violence, where masculinity becomes both a tool and a trap.

Violence with glee

The assumption that psychiatric violence is always done reluctantly or burdened by emotional cost is a comforting fiction. In practice, violence in these settings is often routine, practised, and at times, enjoyed. For those who experience it, particularly racialised women, there is often no mistaking the affective tone with which institutional force is delivered. It is not just that procedures are followed. It is that some men perform them with ease, confidence, and even a quiet satisfaction that speaks of institutional mastery rather than of trauma.

Participant testimonies reveal a pattern in which physical restraint, forced medication, and verbal silencing are not merely tasks but moments of performance. One participant recalled, "He smirked when they called him in. Like he was waiting. He didn't say a word. Just pulled my arm back like he'd done it a thousand times." Another described how a male staff member "always arrived first, always stood in front, always gave the order – he was proud of that." These are not descriptions of men reluctantly enforcing care. These are accounts of men embodying control.

To make sense of this, we must move beyond simple accounts of procedural obligation and attend to how institutions reward and normalise affective detachment. As Ahmed (2010) argues in *The Promise of Happiness*, institutions cultivate emotional orientations – teaching some to remain composed while punishing others for expressing pain or protest. In psychiatric spaces, the expected effect for male staff is one of calm control. Not only must they remain emotionally neutral, but they must also project certainty, distance, and dominance. This posture is not just about safety; it is about legibility as a competent man.

Within this dynamic, some men begin to derive professional identity from the exercise of force. When psychiatric legitimacy is granted through discipline, the ability to suppress resistance becomes a marker of effectiveness. Several participants noted that men who enacted violence efficiently – who "didn't flinch," who "didn't ask questions," who "got it done" – were trusted more, respected more, and given more shifts. The affective detachment that accompanies such acts is not apathy; it is institutional capital.

The pleasure observed in these moments is complex. It is not always sadistic. It is often the pleasure of being recognised, of being needed, of being the man who can resolve a crisis by asserting dominance. Within institutions that deny racialised men many forms of authority, the capacity to restrain, inject, or silence becomes a reliable performance of power. It is not rewarded with a fanfare, but with repetition: more responsibility, more trust, more access.

Hooks (2004) reminds us that patriarchy teaches men to find self-worth not in connection, but in control. "Patriarchy requires of all males that they engage in acts of psychic self-mutilation," she writes, "that they kill off the emotional parts of themselves." In the psychiatric setting, this mutilation is not just internal; it is made manifest through the bodies of others. The woman who is pinned down, the patient who is silenced, and the girl who is injected against her will are not just patients. They are the stage upon which masculinity is made visible.

This does not suggest that all men in these roles enjoy violence. Many do not. But it does indicate that the institution does not require enjoyment to reward repetition. Violence becomes mundane. Control becomes reflex. Some men, particularly those navigating the precarity of post-migration labour, may even find in these acts a twisted form of stability – a way to be useful, to be seen, to be employed.

Participants captured this ambivalence clearly. One reflected, "He wasn't evil. But he liked being called in. It made him someone. In there, he mattered." Another observed, "They never looked shaken after. They joked. They said, 'That one again.' Like it was nothing." These are not outliers. They are reflections of how institutional masculinity is learned, affirmed, and desensitised.

In psychiatric institutions, violence does not require hatred. It requires habit. It requires training. And in some cases, it becomes a site of masculine affirmation not because men hate women, but because the institution teaches them that their value lies in control. That control, once learned, can look like competence. It can even look like pleasure.

Refusal to forget

Where institutions demand obedience, forgetting becomes part of the disciplinary project. The psychiatric system not only manages bodies, but it also attempts to erase memory, to recast resistance as illness, and to silence those who survive it. But memory persists – in the body, in language, and in whispered stories between women who were once restrained and women who still walk with the marks of control. This section is not a conclusion. It is a refusal. A refusal to forget what was done, who did it, and how it felt.

Participants recalled these moments not only in terms of what happened, but in terms of what they meant. The physical pain was often less enduring than the humiliation. One woman described lying in bed after being injected against her will: "It wasn't the injection that broke me. It was the way they walked out like I was nothing. Like I wasn't even there." Another recounted the silence that followed restraint: "After they held me down, no one spoke to me. They just left me. I didn't exist." These are not therapeutic omissions. They are deliberate forms of epistemic erasure.

Hartman (2008), writing of the historical violations of Black women, describes how the archive often fails to capture the textures of pain and resistance. Yet in the face of institutional erasure, she insists on "critical fabulation" – a method of telling stories that were never meant to be told, of remembering what official records were designed to forget. In this context, the stories of women restrained by African male staff, silenced by psychiatric language, and erased through procedure constitute a feminist counter-archive. They are the fragments that refuse closure.

To remember is not only to speak, but it is also to break the institutional pact of silence. The pact that says: if the procedure was followed, no harm was done. The pact that says: if the staff member was Black, it couldn't have been racialised. The pact that says: if he looked like your brother, then your pain must be confusion, not betrayal.

Sharpe (2016) reminds us that memory, especially in the wake of racial violence, is often weathered. It moves through bodies, stories, gestures, and the unspeakable. To remember what was done inside the institution is to carry what it sought to discard. It is, in Sharpe's words, to "tend to the dead and dying" (p.2) in spaces where death is not literal, but symbolic: the death of voice, of selfhood, of agency.

This remembering is a feminist method. As Gordon (2008) has shown, haunting is not simply the presence of what is gone, but the persistence of what institutions try to make go away. The male figure who held down the patient is no longer in the room, but his presence lingers in the flashbacks, in the mistrust of care, in the bodily memory that makes future healing fraught. To name this is not trauma porn. It is political. It is the work of building counter-institutional truth.

Refusal, then, becomes a practice. Not only refusal to comply, but refusal to forget. Refusal to soften the account to protect the dignity of those who enacted harm. Refusal to pretend that patriarchy only lives in whiteness. Refusal to let structural violence be misnamed as unfortunate procedure.

One participant articulated it clearly: "If I forget what he did, it will happen again to someone else. My remembering is my protest."

This remembering is not just an act of healing. It is an act of witness. It is, as Hartman (2008) would say, a way of living in the wake – refusing to accept psychiatric erasure as the final word.

There is no healing to be found in a structure that sees women's resistance as pathology and men's domination as professionalism. Psychiatry, as encountered in this chapter, does not merely mirror patriarchy; it operationalises it. It takes racialised men, many of whom arrive through migratory routes shaped by colonial displacement and economic exclusion, and teaches them to reproduce harm in the name of order. It rewards their detachment, insulates their power, and makes them visible through force.

What this chapter reveals is that patriarchal violence in psychiatric spaces is not always white, not always loud, and not always regretted. Sometimes it is Black. Sometimes it is smiling. Sometimes it is dressed in the uniform of a man whose own life is fractured by precarity, yet who has learned that his safest place in the system is above a restrained woman.

This is the cruel logic of colonial patriarchy: it survives by enlisting the colonised, by asking men of colour to prove their worth through domination, not care. And when women, particularly Black women, refuse to yield and to be quiet and docile, the institution responds by sending in its most loyal soldiers. Men who look like their brothers, their fathers, their neighbours. Men trained to silence, to pin down, to correct.

But this book has not been written for the institution. It has been written against it.

To name what happened is to refuse the scripts psychiatry offer us: that harm was therapeutic; that silence was medical; and that the men who held us down were only following orders. We reject these narratives. We do not seek reform. We do not want better cages. We are naming the system – and the patriarchal afterlives it reproduces – so that we may burn the blueprint and build something else entirely.

To the women who remember: your memory is not inconvenient – it is insurgent.

> To the men who participated: your complicity will not be softened by our silence.
> To the institutions that claim neutrality: your hands are not clean.

And to those still inside: we are working to make an outside that can hold you.I do not write this conclusion as closure. There is no closure for violence that continues. I write it as an opening – to abolitionist care, to community accountability, and to life beyond patriarchal containment. We will not heal in the house of patriarchy. So, we are building elsewhere.

Reflexive questions

1. What forms of violence have I witnessed in psychiatric or institutional spaces that were explained away as "procedure" or "safety?" What did I do in that moment?
2. How does my understanding of "care" change when I hear the voices of those who have been restrained, silenced, or disbelieved?
3. In what ways might I have conflated masculinity with authority, and how has that shaped how I perceive who is fit to lead, to protect, or to heal?

4. Am I more likely to excuse violence when it is enacted by those who share my racial or cultural background? What does that reveal about my own silences?
5. What systems reward me for being distant, compliant, or complicit and what would it cost to refuse that reward?

References

Ahmed, S. (2010). *The Promise of Happiness*. Durham, NC: Duke University Press.

Connell, R. W. (1995). *Masculinities*. Berkeley: University of California Press.

Fanon, F. (1952). *Black skin, white masks*. Translated by C. L. Markmann. Reprint, London: Pluto Press, 2008.

Fernando, S. (2017). *Institutional racism in psychiatry and clinical psychology: Race matters in mental health*. 2nd edn. Basingstoke: Palgrave Macmillan.

Gordon, A. F. (2008). *Ghostly Matters: Haunting and the Sociological Imagination*. 2nd edn. Minneapolis: University of Minnesota Press.

Gordon, L. (1997). *Her Majesty's Other Children: Sketches of Racism from a Neocolonial Age*. Lanham: Rowman & Littlefield.

Hartman, S. (2008). Venus in two acts. *Small Axe*, 12(2), 1–14.

hooks, b. (2004). *The Will to Change: Men, Masculinity, and Love*. New York: Washington Square Press.

Oyěwùmí, O. (1997). *The Invention of Women: Making an African Sense of Western Gender Discourses*. Minneapolis: University of Minnesota Press.

Sharpe, C. (2016). *In the Wake: On Blackness and Being*. Durham, NC: Duke University Press.

Wilson, K. (2012). Race, gender and neoliberalism: Changing visual representations in development. *Third World Quarterly*, 33(2), 303–328.

Wynter, S. (2003). Unsettling the coloniality of being/power/truth/freedom: Towards the human, after man, its overrepresentation – An argument. *CR: The New Centennial Review*, 3(3), 257–337.

5

Estranged minds: Migration, madness, and institutional abandonment

The foreignness experienced by immigrant women in psychiatric institutions is layered and complex. It is not confined to geography, their accent, or their passport. Rather, it is reproduced within institutional routines that pathologise difference and reward docility. For some, foreignness begins before arrival and is shaped by the violence of displacement, the loss of kin, and the precarity of immigration status. For others, it is produced internally as a result of being moved across counties, uprooted from familiar communities, and rendered unrecognisable in institutional settings.

Foreignness is also temporal. It stretches across time zones and memories, creating dissonance between who one was and who one is allowed to be under in the care system. For those born in the UK but racialised as Other, foreignness becomes an imposed identity: the refusal of full belonging despite national proximity. In psychiatric settings, this foreignness becomes clinical evidence. It is interpreted as detachment, irrationality, or non-compliance. The woman who misses her son is sedated; the one who speaks in her mother tongue is labelled incoherent.

To theorise this, I draw on intersectionality (Crenshaw, 1991) as a diagnostic tool rather than as a diversity add-on. Psychiatric harm is not experienced in the same way by all. Race, migration status, gender, language, and class shape who is believed, who is drugged, and who is discarded. Lorde (1984) reminds us that our silences will not protect us – but psychiatric institutions have weaponised silence as survival. We must now ask: what happens when the institution becomes the site where a person's voice is most dangerous?

This analysis is also indebted to diasporic feminist thinkers such as Brah (1996), Spivak (1988), and Anzaldúa (1987), who foreground the psychic ruptures and epistemic challenges of migration. Brah's work on diaspora helps frame foreignness as a structure of feeling: not just a spatial location but a condition of dislocation and longing. Spivak's concept of the subaltern reminds us that immigrant women are often unheard not because they are silent, but because dominant structures are unequipped to hear them. Anzaldúa's notion of the "borderlands" illuminates how women inhabit multiple cultural registers simultaneously; they are rendered incoherent by the institutional refusal to recognise hybrid subjectivities rather than by any lack of clarity on women's part.

For many immigrant women in psychiatric institutions, the harm is ontological as well as medical. They are not simply patients, but displaced subjects whose experiences are unintelligible within dominant epistemic frames. Their language, memory, and cultural logic are misread as incoherence, their grief as madness. This estrangement, shaped by dislocation and compounded by institutional neglect, forms the foundation of the chapter that follows.

> Institutionalisation as exileI didn't even know where I was – someone said Essex, but no one told me why I was moved here. My family is back home; no one even called to ask me if I was okay.

ParticipanTo be institutionalised as an immigrant woman in a UK psychiatric ward is to experience a layered exile: exile from the nation's imagined community and exile within the institution itself. As Brah (1996) argues, a diaspora is not only a question of physical movement but of psychic rupture, where one's attachments to home, community, and epistemic stability are repeatedly unsettled. Psychiatric institutionalisation compounds this estrangement, offering not sanctuary but erasure.

Where Said's (1978) orientalism shows us how the immigrant is cast as unknowable, Brah pushes us further: the immigrant woman is not simply seen as "other" but is rendered un-placeable – she is positioned outside both dominant national narratives and the institutional frameworks of care. Her displacement is not just geographic, but ontological.

Administrative relocation being moved across counties and therefore cut off from city-based support networks is more than a bureaucratic necessity. It is a form of therapeutic exile in which the state reproduces social death under the guise of clinical logic. As one participant notes, being sent from Oxford to Essex meant losing all connection to familiarity. But the institutional reading of this movement remains depersonalised, apolitical, and unacknowledged.

In this context, Spivak's (1988) question "Can the subaltern speak?" becomes painfully relevant. The immigrant woman may speak, protest, or grieve but her utterances are often misheard as instability, non-compliance, or psychosis. Her meaning is filtered through epistemic frames that are unfit to receive her. Institutional care functions here not as interpretation but as translation failure: the immigrant woman's language – cultural, emotional, and relational – is rendered illegible within the psychiatric archive.

Moreover, Anzaldúa's (1987) concept of the *borderlands* helps theorise how immigrant women in wards inhabit liminal psychic spaces: they are caught between cultural frameworks, disciplinary regimes, and institutional timelines. They do not simply cross borders; they are held in them. This state of in-betweenness becomes pathologised rather than understood. To exist in multiplicity is to be treated as fragmented.

This is where intersectionality (Crenshaw, 1991) must be re-anchored not just as a tallying of identities but as a critique of structural design. The woman who is Black, migrant, and female is not simply at the intersection of harm, she is its blueprint. Institutionalisation undercuts her visibility while overdetermining her deviance.

Unlike white British patients, who may benefit from family visits or local familiarity, immigrant women often experience what we might call care without witness. There is no advocate to verify their account, no family to demand reconsideration, and no cultural interpreter to contextualise their pain. Their lack of social defence becomes institutional justification for their over-surveillance.

Foucault's (1977) theory of disciplinary power still applies, but here the carceral logic of the clinic intersects with racialised governance and postcolonial silence. What looks like care is a management of displacement. What looks like treatment is often state-sanctioned containment.

Ultimately, this is exile not as metaphor but as infrastructure. It comprises a structure of racialised, gendered, and epistemic abandonment where psychiatric need is displaced by institutional expediency. Here, the woman is neither patient nor citizen but a subject of medical jurisdiction who does not have a political presence.

We must identify this not simply as a policy failure but as a system designed to obscure responsibility. By removing women from their networks, ignoring their histories, and labelling their grief as disorder, the institution performs both ontological violence and bureaucratic disappearance.

And the question remains: *What does it mean to heal in a place designed to forget you?*

Pharmaceutical control as social dismemberment

> They upped my meds when I asked to go home. I wasn't aggressive – I just said I missed my son. They said I was getting "agitated" and needed to be stabilised.
>
> Participant

Pharmaceutical intervention in psychiatric institutions is often framed as a benevolent act that is therapeutic, neutral, and scientific. Yet, for many immigrant women, it becomes a primary technology of silencing and subjugation. Medication is administered not only to manage symptoms but also to render affect, memory, and resistance illegible. Within this regime, "care" is indistinguishable from containment.

Anzaldúa (1987) calls the body a "site of resistance," and rewritten here by institutional logic into a site of dysfunction. The immigrant woman who mourns in unfamiliar ways, who pleads to go home, and who grieves in a language that is not understood is seen as displaying risk rather than as needing support. Rather than interrogating what her emotions signal, institutions reach for sedation. To quiet her is to regulate her.

This racialised tendency to pacify finds resonance in Mbembe's (2003) notion of necropolitics: the state's right not only to control death but to orchestrate the conditions under which certain lives are lived. Medication, in this setting, becomes an administrative form of life management. Its aim is not flourishing, but docility.

Spivak's (1988) critique of the subaltern's erasure plays out here in chemical terms: the woman may speak, but sedation ensures she is never truly heard. She may express pain, but this is swiftly reclassified as pathology. The voice that emerges under medication is flattened, reordered to fit the institution's schema of compliance. In such spaces, pharmacology does not simply intervene on the body; it disciplines the self.

Foucault (1977) theorises the clinic as a site of observation and normalisation, and we must now ask how the psychiatric gaze is filtered through race, migration, and suspicion. The immigrant woman's differences – linguistic, cultural, and psychic – are not things the institution tries to interpret. They become the very justification for her sedation. Here, diagnosis is less a matter of health than of readability. She is "too loud," "too emotional," "too incoherent" – too far from whiteness to be trusted.

This aligns with Carel and Kidd's (2014) reminder that psychiatric diagnosis is never neutral. It encodes cultural assumptions about coherence, temporality, and rationality, assumptions that are calibrated to dominant, Western, often white norms. The immigrant woman is thus forced into a temporal regime that does not recognise the slow grief of dislocation, the silence of spiritual trauma, or the fractured time of asylum and exile.

Pharmaceutical overreach often operates without resistance because of structural abandonment. Women without family or advocates are especially vulnerable. Their lack of visits is interpreted as evidence of severed ties, when it may, in fact, reflect transnational distance or immigration barriers. Without someone to query dosage or demand a review, institutional impunity thrives. Sedation becomes silence becomes submission.

Austerity and staffing crises amplify this dynamic. Medication replaces relational care not because it is better, but because it is quicker. And this is where the critique must land: chemical restraint is not the symptom of a broken system; it is the logic of a system that is optimised to achieve containment rather than a cure.

In this context, pharmaceutical control becomes a practice of social dismemberment. It disconnects the immigrant woman from her memory, her story, and her claim to belonging. As Spivak argues, it renders her untranslatable to the institution. And as Anzaldúa insists, the wound inflicted is not only psychic, it is also cultural, historical, and embodied.

This is not just sedation; it is structural forgetting. As Brah (1996) reminds us, dislocation is psychic, cultural, and ontological rather than merely spatial. And when that dislocation is chemically enforced, the immigrant woman's story is not just silenced, it is amputated from the institutional archive.

The question is not whether the immigrant women will be discharged. It is whether she will return to a self that can still speak.

The immigrant woman as discredited narrator

> When I told them I was a lecturer back home, they said I was delusional. I stopped talking after that.
>
> Participant

The psychiatric system is not neutral; it is epistemically structured to distrust certain voices. For the immigrant woman, especially one of colour, her narrative is often rendered invalid the moment it departs from the institution's dominant scripts. Her memories, aspirations, and claims to dignity are reinterpreted as signs of instability or delusion.

This disqualification is not incidental. When she says she is a teacher, a mother, a former nurse, or a writer, her words are folded into a narrative of illness. This is what we might term testimonial erasure. Drawing from Spivak's (1988) concept of the subaltern and connecting to the scholarship on epistemic injustice (Fricker, 2007; Carel & Kidd, 2014), we can recognise that the immigrant woman is often structurally positioned as a discredited knower: her speech acts are not only doubted but actively repurposed as signs of pathology. Not all voices can be heard within dominant systems; some are structurally unspeakable.

This erasure occurs in multiple registers. First, in clinical encounters where her symptoms are read as culturally confusing or exaggerated. Second, in institutional files where her life story is reduced to risk markers. Third, in ward dynamics, where her silence is mistaken for compliance and her speech for mania. This dynamic reflects what Fanon (1967) called the "racialised body-in-crisis," where colonial histories of inferiority map onto the psychiatric gaze.

Here, we must return to the diasporic condition. The immigrant woman's story that spans borders her home country, journey, arrival, and struggle, but the institution compresses it into a narrow present: illness now. There is no room for history. No space for transnational complexity. In this flattening, the diasporic subject is reduced to symptoms rather than to a situated life. As Gilroy (1993) reminds us, the Black Atlantic is a site of movement, resistance, and memory, none of which are recognised inside the ward.

Thus, the psychiatric institution not only disciplines the body, it also disciplines memory, narrative, and imagination. The immigrant woman learns to withhold, to mistrust her own words, and to self-monitor every disclosure. This is not therapeutic silence. This is silencing-as-survival.

By refusing to believe immigrant women, the system participates in epistemic violence. Their testimonies are not merely doubted; they are used against them. To speak of one's strength, plan, or education is reinterpreted as instability. This inversion reinforces the institution's power to narrate the patient's truth, even in relation to her protest. "Even the white women who were sectioned were listened to more than us," one Black African participant noted. "When I said I had a degree, they smirked. One nurse said, 'That's what they all say.'"

While immigrant women from varied backgrounds face institutional disbelief, Black immigrant women occupy a uniquely discredited position, one deeply rooted in both colonial histories and contemporary systems of epistemic injustice. As scholars like Fricker (2007), Tuana (2009), and Dotson (2011) argue, credibility deficits are not randomly assigned; they follow the contours of race, gender, and power.

Clinical disbelief is not just interpersonal bias, but the outcome of a long historical arc of medical racism. Historical scripts of Black women as hysterical, aggressive, or emotionally excessive are reinscribed in psychiatric contexts. This is not merely about immigration, but also about the afterlife of slavery in the clinical gaze, where Black pain is minimised and Black agency is pathologised. As Hartman (1997) reminds us, the Black female body has long been the site where care and cruelty blur. In psychiatric settings, this history becomes lived again.

To speak as a Black woman is often to be read as resistant or unstable, a dynamic that deepens testimonial erasure and makes narrative justice even more elusive. To contest this, we must centre narrative justice as a critical framework – one that demands not only that voices be heard but that they be believed, situated, and respected. Implementing narrative justice in institutional settings might mean rethinking clinical documentation to include patients' own accounts in their records, training staff to recognise and counteract testimonial injustice, and developing participatory care models that validate lived experience as expertise. Without this, the immigrant woman will remain a ghost in her own record: spoken about and diagnosed, but never truly listened to.

In the next section, I explore how this erasure is sustained not only through discourse but through pharmaceutical and spatial regimes of control.

Surveillance and the racialised gaze

> I asked for a blanket because it was cold, and the nurse wrote down that I was "demanding." I just kept quiet after that.
>
> Participant

The participant's choice to remain silent after being labelled "demanding" points to a subtle, survival-based resistance, a refusal to offer further material for misinterpretation. To fully understand this moment, I interpret observation logs not as neutral records of behaviour, but as technologies of structural control. As Benjamin (2019) and Magnet (2020) argue, institutional surveillance is not solely about safety, but also about categorising, disciplining, and often erasing those deemed inconvenient, difficult, or excessive. In this context, silence becomes a strategy, an attempt to resist being written into a narrative of pathology. As Brah (1996) reminds us, the diasporic condition is shaped by intersecting borders of power, memory, and marginality, rendering the immigrant woman's presence always already suspect. And as Spivak (1988) underscores, the power to record is the power to silence. In the gaze of the institution, even the act of standing still is loaded with meaning.

This surveillance is epistemological as well as institutional. Drawing on Spivak's (1988) theory of the subaltern, I argue that the power to watch is also the power to miswrite. The observation log becomes a site of narrative control, where silence is interpreted as compliance and protest as pathology. In this way, surveillance functions as inscription: the immigrant woman is not only being watched but is also being scripted out of intelligibility.

Brah's (1996) diasporic lens sharpens my understanding. The immigrant woman is read through intersecting borders of suspicion – racial, cultural, and psychiatric ones. Her actions are over-seen but under-understood. She exists in a double bind: hyper-visible to authority but illegible to empathy.

And if, as Anzaldúa (1987) writes, the borderlands are where multiple worlds clash, then institutional psychiatry becomes one such borderland where the immigrant woman's cultural, linguistic, and psychic expressions are read not as layered but as errant. This misreading becomes structural. Her multiplicity is treated as incoherence. Her body is not just seen – it is scanned for deviance.

I call this carceral seeing where surveillance is not only about managing safety but about maintaining epistemic supremacy. In this regime, to watch is to rewrite and to monitor is to mute. And for the immigrant woman, recovery begins with being seen without suspicion rather than with medication.

Carceral time and the loss of future

> They said, "Why do you keep asking about time? You're not going anywhere."
>
> Participant

Time in psychiatric institutions does not pass; it accumulates. It is organised by medication schedules, meal trays, and ward rounds rather than by life events. For the immigrant woman, this dislocation from temporal continuity can feel like an additional detention: a form of bureaucratic suspension where the future is deferred indefinitely.

As one participant explained, "I missed my daughter's first job. No one told me she called." Another recalled, with quiet devastation, "I was not allowed to attend my mother's funeral, so no closure." These are not just omissions; they are ruptures in the temporal and relational fabric of life. They represent what I term *temporal exile*, a condition in which the immigrant woman is severed from meaningful time, from events that mark life and loss, and from moments that provide continuity and healing.

This loss is spiritual and epistemic as well as logistical. By drawing on Anzaldúa's (1987) understanding of borderlands and cyclical time, we can see how time itself is a site of cultural dissonance.

The immigrant woman does not move through linear psychiatric time, but she inhabits diasporic time, grief time, ritual time. Her mourning does not follow clinical phases but ancestral rhythms. When denied access to funerals, prayer, or even phone calls, her mourning becomes disallowed. Her trauma, unacknowledged, is forced inward. The wound remains open because the ritual cannot be completed.

The institution operates through chrononormativity (Freeman, 2010), a logic that demands recovery in weeks, compliance in hours, and silence in minutes. Deviations from this clock are pathologised. Asking too many questions about discharge, wondering about one's children, or recalling a life back home is read as either delusion or resistance. But this is not resistance to care, but a resistance to erasure.

Here, carceral time meets diasporic rupture. The immigrant woman is not just out of sync, but also punished for being out of sync. Her past is inaccessible, her future withheld. As Brah (1996) argues, diasporic identity is shaped by ongoing negotiation with multiple temporalities. Yet the institution flattens these, compressing all memory into symptoms and all hope into non-compliance.

Moreover, what we are witnessing is not simply the loss of family contact but the dismembering of identity through disrupted time. Without ceremony, without context, and without the right to grieve or to dream, the immigrant woman's narrative is placed on pause while her body is held in bureaucratic suspension. This is not therapeutic stasis, but a temporal captivity.

And yet, within this captivity, we must also locate the resistant pulse of non-linear grief. Against the institutional timeline that seeks punctual recovery, the immigrant woman carries memory as rebellion. Her dreams, her prayers, and her refusal to forget her people become acts of survival. In this way, time is not fully owned by the institution. It is cracked open by those who live otherwise.

The question is not whether she will be "well" in eight weeks, but whether she will be allowed to carry her grief, her memory, and her dignity across the temporal borders she never asked to cross.

Towards narrative repair and structural reckoning

> They talked about me in third person even when I was in the room. My file had more voice than I did.
>
> Participant

The psychiatric confinement of immigrant women is not an aberration. It is a patterned expression of how institutions manage racialised, diasporic, and gendered bodies through logics of silence, suspicion, and bureaucratic abandonment. What this chapter has traced – from testimonial erasure to pharmaceutical suppression and from surveillance regimes to temporal exile – is the cumulative operation of institutional power as both epistemic and affective violence.

Drawing on Fricker's (2007) work on epistemic injustice, we see that the immigrant woman is not merely disbelieved, she is also systematically misread, overwritten, and muted. Her speech becomes pathology. Her grief is deemed excessive. Her knowledge, especially when drawn from diasporic or non-Western sources, is marked as incoherent. This is what Dotson (2011) calls "testimonial smothering": when a speaker self-silences in anticipation of disbelief.

These patterns are not accidental. They are scaffolded by what Spivak (1988) terms the subaltern condition – the structural impossibility of being heard within dominant frameworks. The psychiatric institution, with its files and protocols, becomes a site where *power listens selectively* and where listening itself is racialised.

Time, too, is weaponised. The immigrant woman's non-linearity – her cycles of mourning and her layered diasporic past – is made illegible under institutional chrononormativity (Freeman, 2010). Her need to bury her mother, to mark a family ritual, and to dream about home are dismissed as delusions. The ward is not a space of healing but a temporal captivity in which diasporic memory and non-linear grief are rendered incompatible with recovery. As Brah (1996) argues, diasporic lives are shaped by multiple, intersecting borders, including those of time, memory, and belonging.

Under constant surveillance, the immigrant woman's body becomes both visible and unknowable. As Browne (2015) shows, racialising surveillance ensures that immigrant women are hyper-monitored and under-understood. Her standing to pray becomes a clinical event. Her silence becomes interpreted as docility or dissociation. In this context, even stillness is read through suspicion. As Ahmed (2007) and Collins (2000) remind us, racialised femininity is always already coded as deviant, irrational, or excessive.

Medication – presented as care – is often deployed as containment. Drawing on Mbembe's (2003) concept of necropolitics, we can understand sedation not just as a pharmacological intervention but as a state strategy to dull protest, flatten difference, and erase resistance. The medicated body is not simply a patient; it becomes a manageable subject. Anzaldúa's (1987) insight that the body is a site of resistance calls us to ask: what happens when even that site is chemically neutralised?

And yet, even within such regimes, resistance persists. The immigrant woman refuses full erasure. Her whispered prayers, her small refusals, and her memories of dignity are cracks in the institution's totalising logic. As Arendt (1951) warned, bureaucratic systems do not require hatred to enact violence, only efficiency. It is precisely this mundane machinery—comprising observation logs, dosages, and discharge plans—that turns care into carcerality.

What, then, does repair look like?

Narrative repair begins by restoring the immigrant woman's authority as a knower. Not just as a storyteller, but as a theorist of her own experience. Institutions must embed testimonial justice in the form of co-authored records, cultural advocates, trauma-informed documentation practices, and processes that treat memory not as noise but as knowledge.

But justice cannot end with institutional reform. It must move toward what Gilmore (2022) describes as *abolitionist care* – not the withdrawal of support, but the creation of systems that do not depend on punishment, containment, or silence to function. Abolitionist care demands structures that centre dignity: investment in stable housing, accessible language services, legal accompaniment, and diasporically rooted healing. It also demands that institutions be held accountable not just for what they have done, but for what they have consistently refused to acknowledge or make space for. As Lorde (1984) insists, "the master's tools will never dismantle the master's house." We cannot rely on institutional scripts of care, which are steeped in colonial, carceral, and gendered violence, to deliver liberation. Healing must be reimagined on different terms: collective, relational, and non-coercive ones.

In the end, the immigrant woman's survival is not passive; it is insurgent. Her continued presence, her refusal to be silenced, and her insistence on memory are acts of resistance against a system that was never built for her. The task is not to make her legible to the institution but to make the institution answerable to her truth.

Reflexive questions: Reclaiming voices, rebuilding structures

1. Who is believed in your institution and why? When immigrant women share their distress, how are their narratives interpreted and by whom?
2. How does "care" operate in your context? Is it a relational dialogic practice or a system of compliance and containment?
3. What assumptions underpin psychiatric assessments in your setting? Whose behaviours are seen as "normal" and which ones are marked as risks?
4. How do we make space for knowledge outside Western clinical models? What would it look like to centre migrant women's cultural and emotional vocabularies?

5. In what ways might you be participating in or resisting epistemic injustice? How can you shift from documenting patients to co-authoring care?

References

Ahmed, S. (2007). *A phenomenology of whiteness. Feminist Theory*, 8(2), 149–168.

Anzaldúa, G. (1987). *Borderlands/La Frontera: The new Mestiza*. San Francisco: Aunt Lute Books.

Arendt, H. (1951). *The Origins of Totalitarianism*. New York: Harcourt, Brace & Co.

Benjamin, R. (2019). *Race after technology: Abolitionist tools for the New Jim Code*. Cambridge: Polity Press.

Brah, A. (1996). *Cartographies of Diaspora: Contesting Identities*. London: Routledge.

Browne, S. (2015). *Dark Matters: On the Surveillance of Blackness*. Durham, NC: Duke University Press.

Carel, H. and Kidd, I. J. (2014). Epistemic injustice in healthcare: A philosophical analysis. *Medicine, Health Care and Philosophy*, 17(4), 529–540.

Collins, P. H. (2000). *Black Feminist Thought: Knowledge, Consciousness, and the Politics of Empowerment*. 2nd edn. New York: Routledge.

Crenshaw, K. (1991). Mapping the margins: Intersectionality, identity politics, and violence against women of color. *Stanford Law Review*, 43(6), 1241–1299.

Dotson, K. (2011). Tracking epistemic violence, tracking practices of silencing. *Hypatia*, 26(2), 236–257.

Fanon, F. (1967). *Black skin, white masks*. Translated by C. L. Markmann. New York: Grove Press.

Foucault, M. (1977). *Discipline and Punish: The Birth of the Prison*. New York: Pantheon Books.

Fricker, M. (2007). *Epistemic Injustice: Power and the Ethics of Knowing*. Oxford: Oxford University Press.

Freeman, E. (2010). *Time Binds: Queer Temporalities, Queer Histories*. Durham, NC: Duke University Press.

Gilmore, R. W. (2022). *Abolition Geography: Essays Towards Liberation*. London: Verso.

Gilroy, P. (1993). *The Black Atlantic: Modernity and double consciousness*. London: Verso.

Hartman, S. (1997). *Scenes of Subjection: Terror, Slavery, and Self-Making in Nineteenth-Century America*. New York: Oxford University Press.

Lorde, A. (1984). *Sister Outsider: Essays and Speeches*. Berkeley, CA: Crossing Press.

Magnet, S. A. (2020). *Feminist surveillance studies*. Durham, NC: Duke University Press.

Mbembe, A. (2003). Necropolitics. *Public Culture*, 15(1), 11–40.

Said, E. W. (1978). *Orientalism*. New York: Pantheon Books.

Spivak, G. C. (1988). Can the subaltern speak? In C. Nelson and L. Grossberg (eds.), *Marxism and the Interpretation of Culture*. Urbana: University of Illinois Press, pp. 271–313.

Tuana, N. (2009). 'Viscous porosity: Witnessing Katrina', in Alaimo, S. and Hekman, S. (eds.) *Material feminisms*. Bloomington, IN: Indiana University Press, pp. 188–213.

6 Epistemic violence Silencing, pathologising, and denial of knowledge

Institutions not only manage bodies, they also regulate truth. In the context of mental healthcare, this regulation takes the form of epistemic violence: the silencing, pathologising, and erasure of knowledge systems that do not conform to Euro-Western psychiatric norms. This chapter explores how racialised and gendered patients experience this violence, not simply as diagnostic inaccuracy but as a systematic denial of their ways of knowing, interpreting, and surviving the world.

What is deemed "rational" or "delusional" is not neutral. As scholars such as Spivak (1988) and Foucault (1973) have shown, institutions define what counts as knowledge and who gets to speak it. In psychiatric care, these dynamics play out through dismissals of spiritual meaning, cultural idioms of distress, and alternative cosmologies that do not translate easily into DSM categories.

This chapter unfolds in three interconnected movements:

First, it examines how ancestral and spiritual knowledge is framed as pathology.

Second, it explores how silence becomes a survival strategy when a person is under diagnostic scrutiny.

Third, it addresses how institutions deploy epistemic authority to dismiss complaints, flatten cultural meaning, and obscure harm.

By foregrounding participants' accounts, this chapter proves that these are not merely "misunderstandings" or cultural oversights. They are structural mechanisms of control that are rooted in the colonial logic that continue to shape mental healthcare in the UK.

Ancestral knowledge as counter-epistemology

Rather than merely noting the dismissal of cultural belief systems as pathology, this section reframes those belief systems as counter-epistemologies – modes of knowing that challenge the monopoly of Euro-Western psychiatry. Participants did not simply "believe" differently; they inhabited entirely different epistemic worlds shaped by intergenerational memory, spiritual cosmologies, and practices of relational healing.

For instance, one participant described the presence of ancestors as protective, not distressing: "They were watching over me. But to the psychiatrist, that meant I was hallucinating." What emerges here is a fundamental mismatch not only of diagnosis, but of worldview: where patients seek recognition of pain, institutions impose interpretations rooted in control, compliance, and medicalised authority. This disjuncture reveals what scholars like Mignolo (2007) call the coloniality of knowledge: the ongoing suppression of Indigenous and non-Western epistemologies within modern institutions.

Yet, it is not only ancestral or Indigenous cosmologies that face dismissal. Even expressions of Christian belief, when articulated outside of Euro-Western norms, are frequently cast as pathological. Participants who identified as Pentecostal or Evangelical Christians described being treated with suspicion when they spoke of spiritual warfare, visions, or the presence of the Holy Spirit. "They wrote that I had grandiose delusions because I said I'd been touched by God," one participant recalled. Another was told that her belief in witchcraft, as found in Biblical passages such as Exodus 22:18 and Ephesians 6:12, was "dangerous thinking."

These interpretations, widely accepted in African Pentecostal and Charismatic churches, were not marginal but mainstream in participants' communities. Verses such as Ephesians 6:12 "we wrestle not against flesh and blood, but against principalities, against powers…" were not metaphors but lived realities. Another participant cited Revelation 18:23, which warns that "by thy sorceries were all nations deceived," as Biblical recognition of witchcraft's existence. These scriptural references were at the core of their epistemologies. Yet, in psychiatric settings, invoking them was grounds for alarm, not understanding.

In this way, institutional psychiatry does not simply reject non-Christian forms of belief. It polices what kind of Christianity is acceptable because it aligns with sedate, liberal theologies while casting embodied or prophetic expressions as signs of mental disorder. This reflects what Fernando (2017) and Metzl (2010) have termed the racialisation of madness, in which Black and migrant religious worldviews are medicalised through a secular, white gaze. The diagnostic frameworks used often stem from a profoundly atheistic or Enlightenment-rooted worldview, where a belief in supernatural forces – be they ancestral or Biblical – is automatically treated as irrational unless they conform to narrowly defined "respectable" norms.

Such dynamics expose what Gifford (1998) refers to as the colonial disciplining of religion: an institutional refusal to treat Black or non-Western theologies as valid, moral, or sane. The epistemic violence, then, is double-edged. It delegitimises both Indigenous spirituality and the more fervent forms of Christianity that many in the African diaspora hold dear.

Rather than seeing these epistemic frameworks as threats, institutions encode them as dangerous precisely because they resist being known through the clinical gaze. As Fanon (1967) observes, "the colonised subject is always presumed irrational, and thus in need of external correction." This assumption still lingers in contemporary psychiatry, where a belief in spirits or dreams must be either retranslated or erased.

But these alternative epistemologies are not passive victims of erasure. They often carry quiet, powerful forms of resistance. As one woman said: "They didn't believe in my ancestors, but I knew they were with me. That's why I survived." These statements should not be treated as anecdotal; they are evidence of a counter-archive, a hidden transcript (Scott, 1990) of resistance and survival that the institution refuses to accept.

If we frame these belief systems as survivor epistemologies, we not only dignify them, but we also expose the foundational violence embedded in clinical knowledge. In this sense, legitimacy becomes a kind of badge, a symbolic credential that determines whose truths are heard and which ways of knowing are permitted within institutional spaces. This is why several participants described their diagnostic records with deep mistrust. “It’s not me in there,” one woman said of her file. “It’s who they wanted me to be.” Another said, “If you say you pray, you’re hiding something. If you say you see things in dreams, you’re delusional. So, what do you say? You shut up.”

Such silencing is not incidental. It is the method. It is what makes psychiatric care, at times, indistinguishable from coercion. The refusal to hear – and to hear well – is itself a form of violence.

Thus, in the context of mental health institutions, silence is not a symptom; it is a strategy. For many racialised patients, especially women, silence became the only way to retain autonomy in a space that relentlessly pathologised their words, beliefs, and expressions. Participants described silence as resistance rather than submission: it was a choice made under duress, a tool to avoid being misdiagnosed, over-medicated, or sectioned. “They were always listening,” one woman said. “But not to understand. To find something wrong.”

This dynamic reflects what Foucault (1973) terms psychiatric power: a mode of knowledge production that surveils, categorises, and disciplines under the guise of care. In such a system, language is a liability. As one participant recalled, “If I said too much, they’d write it down. If I cried, they’d say I was unstable. If I smiled, I was manic. So, I stopped talking.” Speech itself becomes an evidentiary trap – every utterance a potential trigger for further intervention. The diagnostic gaze is not neutral; it is saturated with racialised and gendered assumptions.

This weaponisation of language is closely aligned with Kristie Dotson’s (2011) concept of testimonial smothering: marginalised individuals withhold or modify their speech because they anticipate epistemic violence, that is, being misunderstood, dismissed, or penalised. Within psychiatric institutions, this form of silencing is not merely defensive but deeply political. It is a refusal to grant the institution further interpretive power.

Further theoretical resonance is found in Gayatri Spivak's (1988) discussion of the subaltern – those whose voices are not simply unheard but are structurally unhearable within dominant discourses. In this case, institutional psychiatry operates as an epistemic filter, rendering expressions of trauma, belief, or cultural identity illegible unless translated into the language of Western biomedicine. Forms, checklists, and standardised assessments leave no space for ambiguity or multiplicity. The institution does not want to listen; it wants to categorise.

Several participants spoke of this contradiction in their daily encounters. One described being invited to "open up" by a nurse, only to have her words weaponised in the next assessment. "They tell you to talk," she explained, "but they punish you when you do." This double bind mirrors what Ahmed (2012) critiques as the institutional smile: the veneer of care that masks the ongoing reproduction of violence. Vulnerability is invited only to be punished.

This reveals a broader institutional preference for manageable narratives – stories that conform to psychiatric templates and reinforce the clinician's interpretive authority. As Fernando (2017) argues, psychiatry continues to bear the imprint of its colonial roots: it flattens complex cultural realities into symptoms and reframes spiritual or political insight as disorder. One participant reflected, "I knew if I spoke of dreams or ancestors, I'd be labelled. So, I didn't."

This strategic withholding aligns with what philosopher Fricker (2007) calls epistemic injustice, where individuals are harmed specifically in their capacity as knowers. Psychiatric silencing is a particularly potent form of this, where the institutional framework systematically disqualifies forms of knowledge it deems irrational, spiritual, or culturally unfamiliar.

Silence, then, is not emptiness. It is epistemic dissent. It is the refusal to be reinterpreted through a lens that does not recognise your truth. As one woman put it, "Silence was the only thing they couldn't misdiagnose."

This strategy of withholding mirrors Scott's (1990) idea of the hidden transcript – the speech and knowledge withheld from dominant institutions but sustained within communities of resistance. Within this framework, silence is not a void but a container. It holds ancestral knowledge, embodied memory, and political critique that the institution cannot digest.

Indeed, silence is a form of survival against what Fanon (1967) described as the colonial compulsion to make the colonised speak, but only in ways that confirm the coloniser's worldview. In psychiatric care, this manifests as an invitation to share that is framed as therapy but structured through domination.

As a conceptual intervention, we might understand this phenomenon as diagnostic disobedience – a quiet form of rebellion against being rendered legible in harmful ways. It is the refusal to participate in a discursive system that reconfigures truth as illness.

Ultimately, to survive the institution is often to resist speaking its language. Silence becomes both a shield and a signal: a way of saying "you cannot know me on your terms."

Telling the story for you: Institutional rewriting and epistemic capture

If silence was a shield, speech was no sanctuary. Participants described how even when they dared to speak, their words were distorted, appropriated, and re-authored by institutional gatekeepers. "I said I missed my grandmother," recalled one woman. "They wrote down 'patient fixated on the dead.'" Another spoke of a comforting dream involving her ancestors; her words were logged as evidence of psychosis. These acts of narrative rewriting were not isolated. They formed a pattern of epistemic capture where the institution consumes patient expression and reprocesses it into clinical data, often against the speaker's intent.

This practice echoes what Rhodes (2004) calls chart talk: the bureaucratic scripting of patients' lives that reduces complexity to pathology. It's not just that institutions fail to hear racialised patients, it's that they substitute their own meanings in place of the speaker's truth. Speech becomes data, and that data becomes risk. As one participant noted, "It was like they were writing a script. And I didn't get to edit it."

Alcoff (1991), a philosopher, warns of the violence in "speaking for others," particularly when the speaker is institutionally authorised. In psychiatric contexts, this "speaking for" is not just paternalistic; it is disciplinary. What patients say is not merely reinterpreted but absorbed and weaponised. As Hartman (1997) explains in her critique of the archive, dominant institutions often narrate Black suffering in ways that reinforce power rather than disrupt it. Psychiatry, here, becomes an archive of altered voices.

Trouillot (1995) terms this process silencing, achieved through replacement as well as through erasure: the dominant record overwrites the original, often irreversibly. Clinical files are not neutral; they are carceral texts – they follow patients into courtrooms, immigration interviews, child custody cases, and employment tribunals. These files often carry more institutional weight than patients' own voices. "I didn't recognise myself," one participant said. "They took my words and made me sound crazy."

This is epistemic violence in action, the systematic disqualification and substitution of marginalised people's knowledge with state-sanctioned "truth." In her work on testimonial injustice, Fricker (2007) describes how the marginalised are denied credibility as knowers. But in psychiatry, the harm is doubled: not only are patients denied credibility, they also are rewritten into a narrative they can't control. The diagnosis becomes a narrative passport that travels without their consent.

These narratives disproportionately impact those already marked by racialisation, gender, migration status, or class. Skeggs (1997) observes how working-class women's lives were reframed through middle-class moral codes in social work. In psychiatric settings, similar dynamics play out, with white, secular, and biomedical norms defining what is sane, moral, or real. Institutions claim neutrality, but what they demand is conformity to a narrow epistemic order.

This is not incidental; it is inherited. As Fanon (1967) notes, colonial psychiatry was never designed to heal the colonised. It was designed to classify, manage, and punish deviation. The contemporary institution, though differently clothed, continues to demand that patients narrate their lives in its language – or be pathologised.

In this light, we might frame the process not only as epistemic capture but as diagnostic colonisation: the extraction and remoulding of patient narratives to uphold institutional control. What begins as a story of survival or spirituality becomes a note in a file – a warning, a flag, a justification for restraint.

One participant put it plainly: "They didn't just take my voice. They used it against me." This betrayal is not symbolic; it is operational. It shapes who is believed, who is medicated, who is sectioned, and who is listened to. In psychiatry, to speak is to risk being rewritten.

Complicity and betrayal: Proximity without solidarity

For many participants, the deepest injuries were not always inflicted by distant strangers or visibly racist clinicians; sometimes, they were inflicted by those closest in proximity. Porters, care workers, and even nurses who shared the patient's race, language, or migration background were frequently described as enforcers of institutional violence. These encounters felt like betrayals. "It's one thing when it's a white doctor," one participant explained. "But when it's someone who looks like me, who understands where I come from – and they still treat me like nothing? That stays with you."

This betrayal is structural rather than merely interpersonal. As Fanon (1967) warned in *Black Skin, White Masks*, the colonial enterprise survives through the complicity of those it subjugates. Under conditions of racial capitalism, proximity to power often comes at the cost of solidarity. Workers racialised as Black or Brown, particularly migrants in low-waged roles, may enact discipline not out of malice but to survive, and they are trained, incentivised, and surveilled by the institution itself.

This dynamic echoes Farris's (2017) theory of femonationalism, where migrant women are absorbed into care economies not to be empowered but to police others in ways that reproduce Western liberal norms. These workers are expected to display loyalty to the institution, not to those who share their marginalisation. In this framework, relational betrayal becomes a condition of employment.

The betrayal also operates at the level of moral confusion. Participants described moments when they hoped for kindness from a cultural peer, only to be disciplined instead. This moral reversal, where the familiar becomes punitive, compounds trauma. The institution's power lies in its ability to invert care into control and intimacy into regulation. One participant described being forcibly medicated by a nurse who spoke her native language: "She told me to be quiet, that I was embarrassing myself. I wasn't even shouting. Just crying."

Ahmed (2012) describes institutional diversity as a performance that conceals power rather than transforms it. In mental healthcare, diversity among staff often serves as optics rather than as a mechanism for cultural safety. The presence of Black or migrant staff becomes an alibi for the institution, even as it sustains practices of coercion.

This is what Freyd (2018) terms institutional betrayal – when institutions, or those who represent them, violate the trust placed in them by individuals in vulnerable positions. These betrayals are not incidental. They are built into how institutions manage compliance, distribute authority, and reward assimilation.

Even patients knew the cost of disobedience. "They were all scared to lose their jobs," one woman said. "So they chose the institution over us." This is the logic of racial governance: minoritised workers must discipline their own to remain employable.

Yet, complicity should not be misunderstood as consent. As Harney and Moten (2013) argue in *The Undercommons*, those embedded within institutions often navigate impossible choices; they are caught between survival and subversion. Migrant workers especially are burdened by precarious contracts, immigration fears, and surveillance. To appear "neutral" often means to enforce. Neutrality, particularly in institutional care, is not the absence of power but a modality of it. It permits staff to disavow responsibility while still upholding systems of control, rendering detachment a disciplinary tool masked as professionalism.

This complicity does not absolve such migrant workers. But it invites a more layered understanding of power, one where betrayal is not always rooted in hatred but is sometimes grounded in structural co-optation. Institutions recruit those who are marginalised into roles that require them to forget, ignore, or repress what they know to be true. As one participant put it: "She looked me in the eye like she didn't know what it felt like. But she did. She just couldn't afford to remember."

Complicity, then, is not just about what one does; it is about what one is forced to forget. It is the institutional production of amnesia, of moral injury masked as professional duty. In this space, betrayal becomes routine, even rationalised.

Still, the effects are devastating. The betrayal by those closest in proximity carries a particular sting. It undercuts the promise of solidarity, collapses cultural kinship, and renders the institution all-powerful. If the person who shares your story becomes your silencer, where can you speak?

The institution succeeds not only by managing bodies, but by isolating individuals and weakening collective bonds. In such spaces, complicity becomes the condition for being tolerated, while betrayal – of fellow patients, of one's own discomfort – becomes the means of survival. Community is not just eroded; it is strategically undone.

Intersecting harms: Race, gender, class, and the diagnostic gaze

While epistemic violence is often discussed in general terms, the lived realities of participants in this study reveal how systems of power do not operate in isolation. Instead, they intersect, accumulate, and intensify. This intersectionality, first named by Crenshaw (1989), helps us understand how race, gender, class, religion, and migration status collectively shape psychiatric encounters.

Women of colour in this study were not simply subjected to one form of misrecognition. Rather, their identities exposed them to multiple, overlapping harms. A working-class Black woman who speaks of spiritual beliefs is not only racialised but often feminised as irrational, pathologised as lower class, and dismissed as culturally deviant. These layers are not additive; they are synergistic, producing distinct forms of institutional scrutiny.

Collins (2000) describes this as a matrix of domination – a social framework where structural, disciplinary, hegemonic, and interpersonal power converge to regulate marginalised lives. In the psychiatric context, this matrix is evident in the way Black Pentecostal women are disbelieved when they speak of visions, or how South Asian migrants are treated with suspicion when their expressions of distress are culturally encoded.

Even among staff, these dynamics persist. A migrant nurse or care assistant may face her own institutional vulnerabilities, yet may also reproduce harm towards patients in a bid to demonstrate professionalism, assimilation, or authority. The pressures of proximity without power lead to contradictions in which survival for one group becomes punishment for another.

Sociologist Nira Yuval-Davis (2006) reminds us that belonging is not only about inclusion, but also about the conditions under which people are allowed to belong. In psychiatric care, women of colour are often only conditionally recognised as patients if they perform distress in ways legible to white, middle-class norms.

Arendt's notion of the *banality of evil* also offers insight (Arendt, 1963).institutional agents often participate in systems of harm through their ordinary roles and routine duties rather than out of malice. Bureaucratic neutrality becomes the perfect veil for epistemic violence.

These intersectional insights move us beyond the question of bias to one of structure. Psychiatric diagnosis and treatment protocols are not just flawed because of individual prejudice, but they are also embedded in regimes that were never designed with racialised, spiritual, disabled, or poor women in mind. Instead, they become tools of classification and containment.

It is in this context that epistemic violence becomes more than an abstract concept. It is a daily, embodied reality – a force that disciplines speech, rewrites identity, and authorises control. Only by naming the full spectrum of intersecting harms can we begin to challenge the legitimacy of the diagnostic gaze.

Not all madness looks the same: Comparing epistemologies of care

A critical comparison between Western psychiatric frameworks and epistemologies from the Global South helps to reveal the imperial architecture of mental health institutions. In many Indigenous, African, or diasporic traditions, mental, emotional, and spiritual distress is understood relationally and communally, not as an individual pathology. These systems are rooted in cosmologies that recognise dreams, ancestors, spirits, and collective responsibility.

By contrast, Western psychiatry has historically privileged individualism, biomedical reductionism, and Cartesian dualisms of mind and body. It dissects what many Global South traditions hold as interwoven. For example, the idea that an ancestral visitation in a dream could be healing or instructive is seen in many

African contexts not as illness but as wisdom or responsibility. Yet, within Western frameworks, such a statement becomes a clinical red flag – evidence of delusion or mania.

Fernando (2017) warns against the globalisation of Western psychiatry under the guise of universal mental health models, noting how these frameworks often override local knowledge systems. The Global Mental Health movement, for instance, while well intentioned, often promotes models that pathologise non-Western epistemologies and enforce pharmaceutical solutions to what may be social, spiritual, or political crises.

Thiong'o (1986) and Ramphele (1998) both stress the decolonisation of knowledge and care systems as essential for postcolonial liberation. Their insights illuminate how psychiatric institutions function not only as sites of healing but as technologies of governance where knowledge is filtered through imperial values. This creates a double injury: first through marginalisation and then through enforced illegibility.

The epistemologies of care in many Global South traditions embrace ambiguity, ritual, and storytelling. Healing is not linear, and diagnosis is not definitive. Instead of chemical restraint, communities may respond with song, fasting, prayer, or social reintegration. Psychiatric systems, however, treat these approaches as irrational or unscientific.

By comparing these frameworks, we see that what is often framed as care in the West is deeply embedded in surveillance and control. The diagnostic gaze is not a universal tool; it is a cultural product.

As such, the inclusion of Global South epistemologies is a matter of justice rather than of representation. Unless we centre these ways of knowing and being, psychiatry will continue to function as a site of epistemic violence, erasing not only what people suffer from but also how they survive.

Conclusion: Refusing epistemic subjugation

This chapter traced the layered workings of epistemic violence in psychiatric systems: how silence is weaponised, speech rewritten, identities distorted, and entire cosmologies erased. We have seen how institutions do not simply fail to hear; they actively overwrite. Through diagnostic listening, narrative capture, and intersectional harms, psychiatric regimes operate as colonial continuities that are cloaked in therapeutic language. The diagnostic gaze, though framed as care, enforces legibility on terms that erase alternative ways of knowing, healing, and existing.

Yet, within this apparatus of control, we witness acts of refusal. Strategic silence, diagnostic disobedience, and testimonial withdrawal are not symptoms of broken minds but strategies of survival. They are critiques embedded in practice, carried out not in lecture halls or journals but in whispered choices, withheld words, and stories shared only in safe company. These refusals tell us that psychiatry's violence is not complete. There remains resistance, however quiet, in the refusal to comply with epistemic capture.

Importantly, intersectionality reminds us that no single axis explains this violence. It is not merely about race, gender, class, or belief but also about their convergence. Psychiatric violence is not evenly distributed; it is densest where these identities intersect.

This demands that we do more than diversify mental health systems. We must dismantle the foundations that make certain ways of being unrecognisable and certain people permanently suspect.

Using the comparative lens of Global South epistemologies of care reveals that Western psychiatry is not the universal standard it claims to be. Its logic of separation, individualism, and medicalisation are specific, not neutral. And although psychiatry refuses ambiguity, many Indigenous and diasporic traditions make space for it, honouring complexity, spirituality, and community in ways that institutional models cannot.

To imagine equitable mental healthcare is to begin with epistemic humility. It is to centre those who have been silenced, not simply as patients but as theorists of their own survival. As Arendt cautioned, the greatest danger lies not only in overt brutality but also in the bureaucratic routines that make violence feel ordinary. Challenging this ordinariness requires us to name what has been discredited, listen to what has been dismissed, and honour what has been called delusion.

Refusing epistemic subjugation is a political and spiritual imperative as well as an academic task.

Living with the rewrite

I have examined how racialised and spiritualised speech is managed, rewritten, and silenced in institutional psychiatry. Through epistemic violence, testimonial smothering, and diagnostic colonisation, patients, especially women of colour, are rendered simultaneously hyper-visible and unhearable. Their truths are not just ignored but are reformulated in ways that justify control.

We have seen that silence is not absence but strategy. That faith is not delusion but epistemology. And that the badge of care often conceals the machinery of discipline. These insights point to the urgent need to re-theorise psychiatric listening – not as a therapeutic good, but as a form of power.

This raises urgent questions:

Who is allowed to speak and be believed?
What forms of knowledge are legible within psychiatry?
How do systems produce complicity among those tasked with care?
Can we imagine a therapeutic encounter that does not begin with suspicion?

These questions do not close the chapter. They open the next one.

As one participant said: "They tried to tell my story. But I'm still here, and I'm telling it now."

This chapter has attempted to honour the act of telling, not as a gesture of healing or recovery but as a form of refusal: a refusal to be silenced, a refusal to narrate experience in the language of the institution, and a refusal to make pain palatable for systems that caused it.

Reflexive questions for practitioners and scholars

1. What assumptions do I bring into clinical or institutional spaces about who is "sane," "rational," or "truthful?"

   Reflect on how these assumptions may be rooted in racial, cultural, or gendered biases.

2. In what ways might I be participating in epistemic violence – intentionally or unintentionally – through documentation, diagnosis, or silence?

   Consider how routine practices like note-taking or interpreting behaviour may reinforce harm.

3. Whose voices are considered credible in institutional contexts, and whose are dismissed or rewritten?

   How do power and positionality shape what gets counted as evidence?

4. What would it mean to truly "listen" in a psychiatric or institutional setting without the impulse to categorise or explain away?

   Explore alternative forms of listening that allow space for ambiguity and spiritual meaning.

5. How might institutions, and those who work within them, begin to reckon with complicity and move beyond performative inclusion towards relational accountability?

   Think critically about your role within systems of care and control.

References

Ahmed, S. (2012). *On Being Included: Racism and Diversity in Institutional Life*. Durham, NC: Duke University Press.

Alcoff, L. (1991). The problem of speaking for others. *Cultural Critique*, 20, 5–32.

Arendt, H. (1963). *Eichmann in Jerusalem: A Report on the Banality of Evil*. New York: Viking Press.

Collins, P. H. (2000). *Black Feminist Thought: Knowledge, Consciousness, and the Politics of Empowerment*. 2nd edn. New York: Routledge.

Crenshaw, K. (1989). Demarginalizing the intersection of race and sex: A Black feminist critique of antidiscrimination doctrine, feminist theory and antiracist politics. *University of Chicago Legal Forum*, 1989(1), 139–167.

Dotson, K. (2011). Tracking epistemic violence, tracking practices of silencing. *Hypatia*, 26(2), 236–257.

Fanon, F. (1967). *Black skin, white masks*. Translated by C. L. Markmann. New York: Grove Press. (Original work published 1952).

Farris, S. R. (2017). *In the name of women's rights: The rise of femonationalism*. Durham, NC: Duke University Press.

Fernando, S. (2017). *Institutional Racism in Psychiatry and Clinical Psychology: Race Matters in Mental Health*. Cham: Palgrave Macmillan.

Foucault, M. (1973). *The Birth of the Clinic: An Archaeology of Medical Perception*. London: Tavistock.

Freyd, J. J. (2018). *Blind to betrayal: Why we fool ourselves we aren't being fooled*. Hoboken, NJ: John Wiley & Sons.

Fricker, M. (2007). *Epistemic Injustice: Power and the Ethics of Knowing*. Oxford: Oxford University Press.

Gifford, P. (1988). *African Christianity*. London: Hurst.

Hartman, S. (1997). *Scenes of Subjection: Terror, Slavery, and Self-Making in Nineteenth-Century America*. Oxford: Oxford University Press.

Metzl, J. M. (2019). *Dying of whiteness: How the politics of racial resentment is killing America's heartland*. New York: Basic Books.

Mignolo, W. D. (2007). 'Delinking: The rhetoric of modernity, the logic of coloniality and the grammar of de-coloniality', *Cultural Studies*, 21(2–3), pp. 449–514.

Ngũgĩ wa Thiong'o (1986). *Decolonising the Mind: The Politics of*

Ramphele, M. (1998). *Across boundaries: The journey of a South African woman leader*. New York: Feminist Press at the City University of New York.

Rhodes, L. (2004). *Total confinement: Madness and reason in the maximum security prison*. Berkeley: University of California Press.

Scott, J. C. (1990). *Domination and the Arts of Resistance: Hidden Transcripts*. New Haven: Yale University Press.

Skeggs, B. (1997). *Formations of Class and Gender: Becoming Respectable*. London: Sage.

Spivak, G. C. (1988). Can the subaltern speak? In: C. Nelson and L. Grossberg (eds.), *Marxism and the Interpretation of Culture*. Urbana: University of Illinois Press, pp. 271–313.

Trouillot, M. (1995). *Silencing the Past: Power and the Production of History*. Boston: Beacon Press.

Yuval-Davis, N. (2006). Belonging and the politics of belonging. *Patterns of Prejudice*, 40(3), 197–214.

7
Levelled Institutional flattening of memory, identity, and agency

This chapter interrogates the operation of psychiatric wards as sites of institutional control where distinctions between individuals, particularly along lines of race, gender, class, and social role, are flattened under the guise of therapeutic neutrality. Building on previous chapters that explores the structural and epistemic violence experienced by racialised women in the UK systems of care and discipline, this chapter turns to the specific environment of the psychiatric ward as a key site of enforced conformity and depersonalisation.

Grounded in intersectional theory (Crenshaw, 1989; Collins, 2000) and drawing on Goffman's (1961) work on "total institutions," this chapter explores how the ward enacts what Spivak (1988) refers to as epistemic violence – silencing and discrediting the knowledge and voices of marginalised women. Institutional routines, seemingly neutral, serve to erase individuality, regulate emotion, and pathologise deviation from normative expectations of behaviour and recovery. This logic, as Foucault (1977) theorises, operate through the surveillance and regulation of bodies under the guise of medical care.

This analysis is situated within the broader critiques of racial capitalism and carceral governance, attending particularly to the experiences of Black and Brown women whose identities are frequently misrecognised or overwritten by diagnostic categories. Informed by critical disability studies and Black feminist scholarship, this chapter offers a sustained analysis of how institutionalised mental healthcare becomes a site where difference is not attended to but is neutralised – where the complexity of patients' social lives, spiritual frameworks, and epistemologies are rendered illegible.

By centring how gendered, racialised, and classed hierarchies shape experiences of surveillance, participation, speech, and recovery, this chapter contributes to a growing body of scholarship on the racialisation of psychiatric care (Fernando, 2017; Metzl, 2009) while also drawing from institutional ethnography and insider knowledge. The chapter argues that institutional "levelling" is not a symptom of poor care but a structural outcome of a system built to manage, contain, and depoliticise suffering.

Erasing identity through institutional routines

Psychiatric ward routines are rigidly timed and universally applied. Wake-up calls, mealtimes, medication rounds, and group activities are scheduled with minimal flexibility, reinforcing an institutional rhythm that overrides individual preference.

Personal routines, spiritual practices, and cultural customs are rarely accommodated. Patients are expected to eat at set times, queue silently for medication, and sleep at predetermined hours, regardless of personal sleep patterns, dietary needs, or cultural practices. This imposition of standardised behaviour undermines autonomy and expresses what Foucault (1977) identifies as disciplinary time: the organisation of bodies according to institutional needs, not human ones.

These routines are not merely administrative. They function ideologically by recoding difference as disorder. For instance, a Black woman who speaks a different language or plays music in her native tongue may be viewed as disruptive rather than expressive. Patients speaking to relatives in their own vernacular are often interrupted or silenced under the pretext of maintaining a quiet or orderly ward. One woman said, "I was on the phone to my mum, just catching up in Shona, and the nurse came over and said, 'Keep it down, people can't understand you.' As if speaking my own language was something to be ashamed of." In this context, linguistic and cultural difference becomes coded as noise; it is challenged and chastised rather than embraced. Goffman's (1961) concept of "the stripping of the self" is evident in the suppression of these differences – patients must conform to institutional norms in appearance, behaviour, and interaction.

Restrictions on hair products and even basic personal grooming items significantly limit self-expression. This particularly affects women from racialised backgrounds for whom their dress, hair, and body care are deeply tied to cultural identity and dignity. For Black women especially, the impact of prolonged confinement is visibly intensified. After weeks or months without access to protective hairstyles, suitable hair products, or appropriate grooming tools, their hair often becomes dry, matted, or unrecognisable. This deterioration, though entirely preventable, can reinforce harmful stereotypes of neglect or instability. One of the participants said, "By the second month, my hair looked nothing like me. I didn't feel like myself. One of the nurses actually said, 'You're looking wild today.' I just smiled, but inside I was crushed."

As Banks (2000) argues, the visual devaluation of Black hair is deeply rooted in colonial and Eurocentric beauty hierarchies. In the ward context, this neglect is not superficial; it becomes another axis through which respectability and legibility are denied. Moreover, basic grooming activities often become sites of humiliation, as healthcare assistants are known to taunt or belittle patients under the guise of care: "One of the assistants laughed and said, 'Did you forget how to use a comb?' when I asked for a hairband. They think it's funny, but it's humiliating."

Meals and hygiene routines are equally depersonalised. Food is mass produced and lacks cultural variety; bathing schedules and toiletry rations are tightly controlled. These decisions, while justified as matters of safety or efficiency, result in daily micro-erasures of personhood. Black and Brown women often report additional scrutiny during these activities – monitored more closely for contraband or being questioned more frequently about their hygiene practices. One of the women I interviewed said, "They watched me every time I showered. Always checking what I had with me. One day they even opened a new bar of soap I had just brought and said I couldn't use it."

These dynamics exemplify Collins's (2000) analysis of controlling images and the long-standing pathologisation of Black womanhood.

Therapeutic activity, such as knitting, word games, and sewing, is often presented as rehabilitative. However, these daily tasks are rarely optional. Participation is not treated as a choice but as a measure of compliance. Refusing to engage in these activities, even when they lack personal relevance or cultural resonance, is documented as withdrawal or deterioration: "Every morning it was knitting or word search. I said I didn't feel up to it and they wrote, 'Patient withdrawn, not engaging.' It's not therapy – it's a checklist." These routines are better understood through what can be theorised as affective regulation, a system where compliance is not just behavioural but also emotional. Participation, smiling, and passive engagement in routine activities become institutional signs of progress, echoing Ahmed(2012) critique of "institutional happiness." The ward enforces not only bodily discipline but emotional performativity, rewarding those who enact docility while pathologising emotional resistance. As one woman put it, "One nurse told me, 'You seem much better today – you were smiling in the group.' But I wasn't better. I was just tired of being watched."

These practices reproduce Foucault's (1977) analysis of disciplinary regimes that condition the body through repetitive acts of conformity.

Erasure, then, occurs not only through diagnostic labels or clinical notes but through the ordinary operations of institutional life. What appears routine is deeply political. The psychiatric ward's reliance on uniform procedures reflects broader patterns of racial and gendered discipline within state institutions. By flattening complexity into standardised care, the ward systematically silences the very identities it claims to rehabilitate.

What emerges is a logic of clinical neutrality as epistemic violence. Neutrality, in this context, does not signify impartial care but the active refusal to recognise non-dominant expressions of distress, resistance, or healing. By insisting on sameness in experience and response, the ward delegitimises the sociopolitical roots of distress and positions resistance as deviance. In doing so, it upholds a colonial and carceral model of care, one that disciplines difference instead of engaging with it.

This institutional logic can be conceptualised as "care without recognition," a framework in which the appearance of care, offered through routines, safety protocols, and monitored activities, stands in for relational acknowledgement or personhood. Patients may be fed, watched, and treated, but they are not seen. Their knowledge is disqualified, their pain bureaucratised, and their resistance translated into pathology. This is not incidental. It is the mechanism by which institutional levelling operates, and survives.

Daily searches and the criminalisation of possession

In psychiatric wards, personal belongings are routinely subjected to unannounced searches, justified as safeguarding measures. Yet these searches function far beyond risk prevention; they operate as tools of surveillance and criminalisation. Feminine hygiene products, intimate clothing, and personal cultural items are treated as suspect, their presence questioned and their use restricted. Black and Brown women report having their bags, clothing, and underwear searched without explanation. Even used or unopened sanitary pads may be rifled through. The logic of containment positions ordinary objects as potential threats, and by extension, the people who own them as inherently dangerous.

This hyper-surveillance is not neutral; it reflects what Browne (2015) terms the "racialised surveillance of Black bodies" within carceral institutions. Possession itself is pathologised; the act of having, protecting, or desiring personal space is rewritten as non-compliance. Here, Foucault's (1977) notion of "docile bodies" is made literal: bodies are stripped not just of agency but of property, comfort, and privacy.

Patients often beg to charge their phones in order to maintain contact with the outside world, only to be ignored or spoken to rudely by staff. Access to phones is tightly controlled; patients must knock at the nurses' desk to request their devices and are frequently dismissed or made to wait. This gatekeeping underscores the hierarchical structure of the ward – those who control communication and time wield disproportionate power.

Healthcare assistants may mock or question the value of personal items, reinforcing the view that only institutional logic matters. This is not simply about the loss of property but is also about what Spivak (1988) describes as epistemic erasure: the removal of cultural knowledge and self-determined meaning. The message is clear: only one way of being, expressing, or healing is legitimate.

Moreover, the search process is often gendered and racialised. Women who attempt to explain the importance of certain items, such as hair grease, religious symbols, or language-specific books, are treated with suspicion. Rather than engaging with the cultural context, staff often pathologise the very need to explain. Requests are interpreted as manipulative; needs become threats.

Beyond physical searches, the staff presence itself becomes a form of surveillance. Healthcare assistants routinely walk up and down the corridors, peering through windows and cracks in doors, which interrupts rest and privacy. Even times of solitude – lying in bed, reading, and reflecting – are disrupted by constant movement and presence. The ward becomes a space where even silence and stillness are interpreted, recorded, and managed. This intensifies the loss of interiority and the ability to retreat from public gaze, especially for women already subjected to racialised readings of emotion and behaviour.

These dynamics reflect a broader institutional logic we might call affective securitisation: the management of emotion and identity through the control of the material and spatial. It is not only bodies that are regulated but the attachments, meanings, and rhythms of daily life. This form of regulation reproduces the logic of border control within institutional walls, where cultural expression is not a right but a risk and where those who carry difference are positioned as foreign to the institution.

In this way, the psychiatric ward reproduces what Puwar (2004) terms the "space invader" dynamic: racialised bodies that are seen as out of place within white institutional norms. Possession is not only about things; it is also about who is permitted to hold, keep, or value. Under institutional logic, racialised women are not only rendered voiceless but are also stripped of the very materials and time that root them in selfhood.

The search, therefore, is not incidental; it is structural. It enacts the ward's foundational aims: to level, to neutralise, and to remake patients into subjects that fit the institution's narrow scripts of compliance and recovery. What is needed, then, is not merely the reform of policies but a reimagining of what psychiatric care could look like, care that centres autonomy, relationality, and epistemic justice. Change requires more than critique; it demands active undoing of institutional violence and the creation of alternative care models that recognise difference as insight rather than as disorder.

Infantilisation as a compliance strategy

Infantilisation in psychiatric wards is not accidental; it is a central mechanism through which power is asserted and compliance is demanded. Patients are routinely treated as if they are incapable of decision-making. They are stripped of adult responsibilities and autonomy and subject to activities and routines that resemble a schoolroom more than a site of healing. The removal of phones and personal technologies is accompanied by the provision of glue sticks, colouring pages, and simple craft materials. These are not offered as optional pastimes but enforced as therapeutic tools. Participation in such infantilised activities becomes a measure of co-operation. Non-participation is noted, medicalised, and used to reinforce a patient's lack of progress. One participant said, "They handed me wool and needles like it was a lifeline. I said I didn't want to knit, and the nurse just smiled like I was being difficult. 'This is part of your recovery,' she said – as if sewing a cushion would heal years of trauma."

This practice aligns with what Fanon (1967) critiques as the infantilisation of colonised subjects, where autonomy is systematically denied and adult capacities are deliberately diminished to justify control. The psychiatric ward replicates this through what might be called structural belittlement: the reduction of adults, especially racialised women, to having a childlike status under the pretext of safety and healing. Patients are not simply encouraged to engage in therapeutic activities; they are made dependent on institutional approval for the most basic decisions: "If you don't clap during group therapy or smile during bingo, they write it down. One of the assistants said, 'Come on, don't be a spoilsport.' Like I'm in a playground."

Requests to rest, avoid group activities, or speak in one's own language are frequently denied or pathologised. Patients who ask for alternatives to group crafts or knitting may be dismissed as resistant, difficult, or manipulative. Healthcare assistants may mock those who do not participate enthusiastically, interpreting hesitation as a lack of gratitude rather than a legitimate need for different modes of engagement. One woman told me: "I asked to lie down instead of joining their word game. The nurse said, 'If you want to get better, you need to be with the group.' Like resting made me suspicious." These kinds of responses reflect Ahmed(2012) critique of the institutional demand for happiness, a system where emotional compliance is misread as clinical progress.

This infantilisation intersects with what Berlant (2011) refers to as "cruel optimism" – the institutional offer of care that requires submission and loss of agency. Patients are expected to accept humiliation, silence, and trivialisation in exchange for the promise of wellness. Resistance, even in the form of quiet withdrawal, is transformed into evidence of illness. Rest becomes laziness; assertiveness becomes aggression.

Language is a further terrain of infantilisation. Staff often use diminutive words, for example, calling adult women "girls," use overly sweet tones, or instructing them as one might a child. Corrections are issued in public, decisions are made without consultation, and any challenge to authority is met with reprimand. One of the participants described that was used: "She kept calling me 'sweetie' and 'good girl.' I'm a grown Black woman with a PhD. But in here, that doesn't count. You're just a 'girl' again." This linguistic framing is not benign; it is a key mechanism through which power is made to feel natural and resistance is recoded as immaturity.

The cumulative effect is the production of what can be theorised as managed dependency: a condition where institutional control is maintained by framing patients as perpetually incapable. This dependency is not created by illness but by the systematic stripping of autonomy, voice, and adult status. "We had to ask permission to use the toilet after group. I'm not five years old. You start questioning if your body still belongs to you," one woman said. For Black and Brown women, who already navigate racialised assumptions of incompetence or volatility, this infantilisation is compounded by intersecting forms of misrecognition.

Far from being therapeutic, these practices reinforce the institution's authority by rendering difference illegible and autonomy threatening. The demand is not to heal but to submit to a form of recovery that aligns with white, middle-class, normative ideals of femininity and emotional regulation. To be seen as improving is to be seen as quiet, grateful, and small.

Reversing this logic requires more than offering alternative activities. It requires dismantling the underlying structures that conflate dependency with care and replacing them with models that honour autonomy, difference, and self-determination. Infantilisation must be named as a structural form of control rather than a therapeutic misstep and recognised as something that disciplines patients into submission rather than walking with them in recovery.

Sleep within the psychiatric ward is less a biological necessity than an institutional demand. While framed as rest and recovery, ward-imposed sleep routines are governed by the need to render bodies passive and controllable. Drawing on Foucault(1977) theory of disciplinary power, night-time in the ward is revealed not as a period of relief but as another site of regimented surveillance.

Lights are dimmed at scheduled hours, and patients are required to lie in bed regardless of whether they are tired or emotionally settled. Such standardisation enacts what Lefebvre (2004) might describe as the colonisation of everyday rhythms; it imposes externally defined cycles on internal needs. As one participant noted, "They turned off the lights at the same time every night. It didn't matter if you were crying or wide awake. You had to lie there in the dark and pretend to sleep."

This routinisation is underpinned by what Butler (2004) conceptualises as normative performativity: the expectation that patients demonstrate wellness through compliant rest. Refusal to conform, such as staying awake, reading, or quietly engaging in spiritual practice, can be interpreted as non-compliance or deterioration. "One night I sat up to pray quietly and they told me to get back in bed," one woman said. "It was like I wasn't allowed to move unless it was on their terms."

This dynamic aligns with Browne's (2015) theorisation of racialised surveillance, where Black and Brown bodies are disproportionately subjected to the gaze. A participant told me, "You close your eyes for a moment, and you hear them walking past, stopping, scribbling. What could they be writing? That I blinked too much?"

Rather than enabling rest, the night-time environment engenders hypervigilance. The inability to secure personal space – curtains that do not close, doors that do not lock, lights that flicker or remain on in hallways – creates what Fanon (1967) might describe as a condition of nervous exhaustion under systemic oppression. Another woman put it bluntly: "You never sleep properly. You just close your eyes and wait for the door to creak open."

The ward's model of rest thus reinforces a racialised politics of silence and stillness. Stillness is policed; motion is interpreted. In this space, the right to solitude becomes conditional and is always revocable. For women already grappling with histories of trauma, displacement, or systemic marginalisation, the impossibility of uninterrupted rest reflects not just institutional overreach but a fundamental misrecognition of the restorative practices they may need.

Rest, in this context, is better understood as a contested terrain – a site where the state through institutional routines attempts to claim ownership of time, body, and mind. What is needed, then, is a reimagining of rest as political resistance. According to Lorde (1984), rest for those who are marginalised is not a luxury but a necessity, and institutional settings that deny this are complicit in reproducing harm. Until psychiatric spaces reckon with their own power to deny even the most basic expressions of personhood, they will remain mechanisms of erasure rather than sites of healing.

Conclusion: Institutional levelling as structural violence

Institutional levelling in psychiatric wards is not a failure of care but a system that is functioning precisely as it is intended to: to depersonalise, contain, and discipline. Through routine, surveillance, and enforced conformity, these spaces erase cultural identity, suppress resistance, and recode survival strategies as symptoms of pathology. The lived experiences of racialised women within these wards reveal how care becomes coercion that is administered not in the service of healing but in the maintenance of institutional order.

The mechanisms I have described – disciplinary routines, infantilisation, surveillance of rest, and the criminalisation of personal belongings – are not isolated practices but components of a coherent system. The ward functions precisely through banal routines that become mechanisms of epistemic and racialised violence, normalising structural harm under the appearance of order. By drawing on Spivak's (1988) theory of epistemic violence and Foucault's (1977) analysis of disciplinary institutions, we can see how psychiatric wards operate as carceral spaces that produce docile subjects through affective and material control.

This chapter demonstrates that healing cannot occur in environments that deny agency, misrecognise cultural meaning, and pathologise resistance. True reform cannot be limited to improving services within existing frameworks. What is required is a dismantling of institutional logics that treat difference as disorder. This means embracing epistemic justice: centring the knowledge, needs, and survival strategies of racialised women as foundations for new models of care and not as deviations.

The way forward lies in relational, culturally responsive, and structurally aware approaches that honour lived experience and restore dignity. Psychiatric care must move beyond containment and towards recognition of identity, complexity, and the political conditions of suffering. Only then can care begin to mean healing and not harm.

Reflexive questions

1. How does the concept of "institutional levelling" reshape your understanding of standardised care in psychiatric settings?
2. In what ways do surveillance practices in mental health institutions reflect broader social controls enacted on racialised and gendered bodies?
3. How can we, as practitioners, researchers, or community members, work towards epistemic justice in mental health care?
4. What alternative models of care exist – or could be imagined – that honour cultural, spiritual, and communal forms of healing?
5. What would it mean to design psychiatric spaces where rest, resistance, and refusal are not pathologised but supported?

References

Ahmed, S. (2012). *On Being Included: Racism and Diversity in Institutional Life*. Duke University Press.

Banks, I. (2000). *Hair Matters: Beauty, Power, and Black Women's Consciousness*. New York University Press.

Berlant, L. (2011). *Cruel optimism*. Durham, NC: Duke University Press.

Browne, S. (2015). *Dark Matters: On the Surveillance of Blackness*. Duke University Press.

Butler, J. (2004). *Undoing Gender*. Routledge.

Crenshaw, K. (1989). Demarginalizing the intersection of race and sex. *University of Chicago Legal Forum*, 139–167.

Fanon, F. (1967). *Black skin, white masks*. Translated by C. L. Markmann. New York: Grove Press.

Fernando, S. (2017). *Institutional Racism in Psychiatry and Clinical Psychology: Race Matters in Mental Health*. Palgrave Macmillan.

Foucault, M. (1977). *Discipline and Punish: The Birth of the Prison*. Vintage Books.

Goffman, E. (1961). *Asylums: Essays on the Social Situation of Mental Patients and Other Inmates*. Penguin.

Hill Collins, P. (2000). *Black Feminist Thought: Knowledge, Consciousness and the Politics of Empowerment*. Routledge.

Lefebvre, H. (2004). *Rhythmanalysis: Space, Time and Everyday Life*. Continuum.

Lorde, A. (1984). *Sister Outsider: Essays and Speeches*. Crossing Press.

Metzl, J. M. (2009). *The Protest Psychosis: How Schizophrenia Became a Black Disease*. Beacon Press.

Puwar, N. (2004). *Space Invaders: Race, Gender and Bodies Out of Place*. Berg.

Spivak, G. C. (1988). Can the subaltern speak? In: C. Nelson and L. Grossberg (eds.), *Marxism and the Interpretation of Culture*. University of Illinois Press, pp. 271–313.

8
Exiting but not free Surveillance, stigma, and systemic abandonment post-discharge

What is freedom after discharge?

Discharge from psychiatric care is often framed as a moment of triumph – a clinical indicator of stability, a return to self-sufficiency, a re-entry into the social. But for many racialised women, discharge does not mark the end of institutional control; it marks its transformation. The body may be released from the ward, but the logic of the institution travels with it. The gaze follows. The notes follow. The suspicion follows. Freedom, if it comes at all, is partial; it is contingent, watched, and reversible.

This chapter argues that psychiatric discharge is not a moment of liberation but a recalibration of power. The afterlife of institutionalisation lingers in the body, in the neighbourhood, in the workplace, and in the mind. Surveillance doesn't disappear; it decentralises. Care doesn't fade; it becomes more ambivalent, less accountable, and more ghostly. One is no longer under the hospital's jurisdiction, yet one is still not fully reabsorbed into the social. This is not recovery; it is suspension.

The language of aftercare – of "follow-up" calls, "support" plans, and "community outreach" – functions as a bureaucratic grammar that masks abandonment. Under the NHS policy, post-discharge care is structured around minimum obligations rather than relational commitment. Patients are often assigned care coordinators they rarely see, asked to attend meetings that centre compliance rather than conversation, and left to navigate the social wreckage of institutional contact alone. Where was the support when the silence settled in? Where was care when the world no longer made sense, but was no longer allowed to collapse?

This chapter draws on what Piepzna-Samarasinha (2018) describes as the difference between care that is *for control* and care that is *for liberation*. The former checks boxes, enforces routines, and upholds state power, and the latter listens, adapts, and resists erasure. Here, I interrogate how racialised women discharged from psychiatric settings encounter the world not as survivors welcomed back but as liabilities reinserted into systems of soft policing.

To be discharged is not to be done with the institution. It is to carry its shadows into everyday life: in the way neighbours listen too closely, in the way laughter is read as mania, in the way your own voice, if it rises too suddenly, is no longer yours to explain. This chapter does not offer tidy resolutions; instead, it sits in the discomfort of return. What does it mean to be "better" in a world that caused the crisis? What does it mean to be home when home no longer trusts you?

Not everyone left traumatised – They all took something home

Not every woman who left the ward described herself as traumatised. Some articulated a kind of numbness, a dulling of the senses rather than a rupture. Others spoke of managing, of adjusting, of "just getting on with it." But what united all accounts was a quiet acknowledgment: something stayed behind and something else came with them. There was a subtle dislocation. A new mistrust. A bodily knowledge that the world could turn clinical at any moment. This is not trauma in the spectacular sense so often portrayed in media – shaking bodies, intrusive flashbacks, and cinematic breakdowns. It is trauma as residue, something that settles in the bones, in the way one watches oneself speak, in the way certain corridors, colours, or smells suddenly constrict the throat. As Lorde (1984) reminds us, pain that is unnamed does not become less real; it becomes internalised. It becomes a shaping force. For some, what they carried was physical. The neglect and overmedication inside the ward translated into chronic fatigue, nerve damage, or in one participant's case, permanent mobility impairment. The absence of an accessible infrastructure after discharge meant that her new wheelchair became not just a tool, but a marker – a symbol of the institutional harm that went unacknowledged. "I didn't go in disabled," she said. "I came out needing ramps." This is the institutional afterlife that Ben-Moshe (2020) theorises: a continuation of carceral logic beyond walls. It is not only confinement that disables but also the cumulative effect of being disbelieved, oversedated, and dismissed. The very structures claiming to treat mental distress end up producing new layers of debilitation, then retreat into silence after discharge. Others took home an altered social reality. Friends no longer called. Colleagues avoided eye contact. Family members walked on eggshells, offering thin reassurances and quick subject changes. And neighbours? Neighbours listened for madness. "After he screamed," one woman recalled, referring to her husband accidentally burning himself, "they came running – not to help, but to check if I had gone off again." It was a joke, but not really. The assumption lingered in the air like smoke. Here, Goffman's (1961) idea of "spoiled identity" becomes more than a label; it becomes a filter through which all future behaviour is read. Any deviation, any loudness, any silence can be interpreted as regression. This is not simply stigma; it is conditional belonging. You are accepted only to the extent that you perform recovery, manage your emotions, and remain readable within institutional timelines. Participants spoke of becoming experts in self-surveillance. "You start checking yourself before anyone else can," said one woman. "Am I talking too fast? Am I smiling weird? Do I look well enough to pass?" This is the psychic cost of institutionalisation; it means not just being watched, but internalising the watcher. What Ahmed (2012) calls "the promise of happiness" becomes a cruel metric: you must look better, act better, be better, regardless of how you feel or whether healing has even begun. Importantly, not everyone framed their experience as victimhood. Some spoke with defiance or sarcasm, or even with humour. One woman laughed when describing her first day home: "The silence was so loud, I thought the walls were judging me." This refusal to conform to a tragic script is not a denial of pain; it is a strategy of endurance and a refusal to be consumed by the institution's narrative of brokenness. What emerged across testimonies was not a singular story but a fractured archive of embodied knowledge. A collection of interrupted dreams, altered bodies, and guarded conversations. Not everyone left with the same wound, but everyone left marked. Even after discharge, the interpretive gaze of the institution lingers. It follows patients not just into their homes but into their GP (general practitioner) appointments, their casual conversations, and their private moments. Local GPs, meant to serve as primary care providers, often become informal extensions of psychiatric oversight. "I told him I felt down," said one woman, "and he started talking about medication again – like sadness wasn't allowed anymore." This flattening of emotional range, where sadness, grief, or even silence are treated as clinical symptoms, reveals what we might term post-institutional hyperlegibility. This concept captures how individuals, especially racialised women, must perform legibility according to the narrow institutionalised definitions of wellness. Anything outside this frame – talking to oneself, singing in the house, needing quiet – can be read as a sign of "relapse." The body is no longer neutral; it is a site of risk assessment. Post-institutional hyperlegibility builds on Foucault's (1977) theory of disciplinary surveillance and Goffman's (1961) account of the "spoiled identity," but it extends their insights by recognising how diagnostic suspicion migrates into everyday life. In this paradigm, even private actions are pre-interpreted through the lens of pathology. What is harmless, playful, or idiosyncratic becomes evidence of disorder. As one participant put it, "I can't hum a song without wondering if someone thinks I'm mad again." This phenomenon also intersects with what Ahmed

(2012) calls institutional affect: the emotional norms embedded in systems. Institutions do not just regulate what one does but how one feels, and more importantly, how one is seen to feel. In this context, emotional expression becomes a monitored performance. The ward may be gone, but its gaze survives in the eyes of GPs, neighbours, employers, and even loved ones. Importantly, this hypervisibility is racialised. Black women especially are often read through tropes of instability, aggression, or irrationality (Crenshaw, 1989; Collins, 2000). Their emotional expression is less likely to be interpreted as distress and more likely to be read as threat. After discharge, this makes ordinary acts – raising your voice, expressing exhaustion, or simply being – liable to be reinterpreted as clinical risk. This is the afterlife of psychiatric contact: there is no freedom, only a probationary kind of belonging to a world where joy must be measured, silence must be justified, and sadness must be hidden. Where humming to yourself becomes a diagnostic act.

Aftercare or after-control?

Discharge is often framed as a return to autonomy, a symbolic crossing back into "normal life." Yet, for many women, leaving the ward marked not the end of institutional entanglement but a shift in its form. Instead of experiencing liberation, they entered a subtler system of oversight, what we might term administered abandonment: a regime of bureaucratic attention that simulates care while maintaining control.

Under NHS protocols, discharged patients are typically assigned a care coordinator or community mental health nurse. These roles, officially rooted in therapeutic support, often functioned as extensions of surveillance, marked by brief home visits, standardised risk checklists, and medication compliance reviews. Several women described these encounters as evaluative routines rather than as spaces of dialogue or care. "They'd come in, ask two questions about meds, tick the box, and leave," one participant explained. "I stopped answering honestly. It wasn't worth the extra visits."

These processes reflect what Ben-Moshe (2020) describes as part of the carceral continuum: the idea that confinement does not end at the door of the institution but is redistributed through community infrastructures. Discharge, in this model, disperses institutional logic – its suspicion, its risk aversion, and its flattening of complexity – into domestic and social spaces.

This transfer of authority is not merely logistical; it is affective. Former patients reported altering their homes, rehearsing their moods, and monitoring their voices in preparation for these visits. "It felt like Ofsted for your life," one participant recalled. "I'd clean, practise what to say. They weren't checking in. They were grading." This metaphor – inspection, not inquiry – captures the way care became performance.

Where Ahmed (2012) offers the idea of "performative compliance" – appearing well as a strategy for survival – others take this further. Benjamin (2019) speaks of "the New Jim Code," whereby ostensibly progressive systems (including health tech and community care) reproduce racialised surveillance under the guise of innovation or efficiency. In this context, care coordinators act as human algorithms, flagging non-compliance or emotional complexity as threats to be managed rather than realities to be respected.

And those most frequently flagged were not random. Black and Brown women repeatedly described aftercare interactions as steeped in suspicion and paternalism

> "She spoke to me like I was stupid," one woman recalled of her care coordinator. "Like I might go mad at any second."

Another, reflecting on the constant second-guessing of her emotional expression, noted: "If I said I was tired, I was depressed. If I smiled too much, I was manic. There was no safe mood."

These dynamics echo analysis of how controlling images operate, especially against Black women who are simultaneously expected to be resilient and penalised for any deviation from emotional norms. The post-discharge landscape becomes one in which emotional readability is weaponised and where deviation from institutional expectations invites further scrutiny.

Crucially, this so-called aftercare rarely engaged with the broader conditions that shaped women's distress in the first place – racism, precarity, violence, and isolation. Instead, it measured wellness through compliance. "They never asked about my housing," said one woman. "Just if I was taking the tablets."

This is the logic Sharpe (2016) calls "the weather," the totalising, atmospheric violence that surrounds Black life. In this context, aftercare becomes one more mechanism through which that weather is obscured. The individual is made legible only through medical discourse; structural violence is disavowed, dislocated from the diagnostic script.

Even humour, used by many participants as a coping mechanism, was subject to suspicion. "I made a joke once," said one woman, "and she wrote in her notes that I had 'inappropriate affect.' I said, what do you want, tears?"

This is not aftercare. It is after-control, a diffused, depersonalised form of epistemic discipline that masks its violence in the language of welfare. As Ben-Moshe (2020) reminds us, abolition is not just about closing institutions, it is also about refusing the replication of carceral logic in the name of help.

Reimagining care must involve more than policy reform. It requires a radical reconsideration of who is allowed to define wellness, whose voices are believed, and what kinds of support are seen as legitimate. Until then, care will remain conditional. And discharge will remain not an end but a beginning of a quieter, more insidious kind of captivity.

Surveillance without walls

Discharge may mark the end of formal confinement, but it does not mark the end of surveillance. For many, the psychiatric gaze migrates into the community – through neighbours, family members, and local institutions – forming what might be termed as *surveillance without walls*. This is not merely metaphorical. The participants in this study described a climate of social hypervigilance where the legitimacy of their emotional expression, behaviour, and even domestic sounds became subject to clinical suspicion.

This reflects what Ben-Moshe (2020) terms "administered abandonment," a condition where institutional withdrawal does not equal freedom but instead produces new vulnerabilities, enacted through diffuse social controls. It is also echoed in Goffman's

(1961) theory of the "spoiled identity," wherein the individual is not permitted to return to society unmarked. Every future action is filtered through the past diagnosis. Normal variations in emotion or behaviour become subject to clinical interpretation, especially for racialised women.

Participants shared that even ordinary acts – singing, speaking in one's native language, or needing solitude – were policed. "I was told not to talk too loud to my mum on the phone," one woman recalled. "They said it was disturbing others. But it was just our language – it wasn't even loud." Another described being told to turn down her music even though it was no louder than her white neighbour's. The institutional suspicion had merely changed location.

I propose the term "ambient clinicality" to capture this phenomenon: the condition of being socially and clinically readable as a potential patient, even outside the hospital. Unlike formal surveillance, which operates through documentation and staff presence, ambient clinicality is enacted through everyday interactions – looks, questions, and silences – that reinscribe the person into a framework of risk. It is a lived condition of conditional belonging in which presence is tolerated only if it appears normative, silent, and stable.

This burden is unevenly distributed. Black and Brown women often bear the brunt of this ambient scrutiny, which was compounded by racialised assumptions about danger, instability, and emotional volatility. As Crenshaw (1989) and Collins (2000) have argued, the convergence of race and gender amplifies misrecognition. One participant said, "Sometimes I feel like I can't even sigh too loudly. It's like I'm always being assessed – by the street, by the doctor, by my own family."

The cumulative effect is a form of psychic compression. Surveillance without walls produces internalised discipline, compelling women to rehearse normalcy, suppress authentic expression, and question their own instincts. It is not the ward that follows them; it is the epistemology of control, replicated through diffuse social actors.

And yet, participants also wielded humour, irony, and subversion as tools of survival. One woman said, "Now when I catch myself singing to myself, I say it out loud: 'Don't worry, I'm not mad, just vibing.' It's like I have to narrate my sanity." This strategy, while painful, is also a refusal – a way of making visible the absurdity of constant readability.

Thus, post-discharge life is not simply a return to society; it is an entrance into another kind of institution, one dispersed across post-codes, professions, and relationships. If psychiatric wards sought to make patients compliant, the world outside asks them to be legible. And in both cases, failure to comply risks renewed surveillance.

The next section examines the internalisation of these dynamics – how women learn to self-monitor, rehearse their answers, and manage the performance of recovery not for themselves, but for the gaze of others.

The performance of recovery: Internalising the institutional gaze

The transition from patient to citizen is rarely clean. For many women, the formal discharge from psychiatric care marks a shift in disciplinary strategy rather than the end of it. The ward may have receded, but its logic remains embedded in how one speaks, dresses, moves, and emotes. Recovery itself becomes a genre – one that demands performance, often at the cost of authenticity, emotional range, and dignity.

Several participants described this state of "curated wellness," where everyday gestures are filtered through an internalised diagnostic lens. "You start to audit yourself," said one woman. "I practise my answers before I speak. I scan my tone. I plan my smile." This is not mere habit; it is survival under ongoing scrutiny.

Rose's (1999) concept of "responsibilised subjectivity" is instructive here. The neoliberal psychiatric state no longer confines solely through institutions; it produces subjects who internalise risk management. Post-discharge, individuals are expected to self-regulate in ways that reassure others of their "wellness," anticipating suspicion, and performing emotional containment. This form of "psy-visibility" turns everyday life into a site of ongoing assessment.

This psychic labour is deeply racialised. Black and Brown women described the impossibility of showing frustration or fatigue without being labelled unstable. As one woman explained, "I don't have the luxury of being tired. If I don't smile, I'm labelled difficult. If I raise my voice, I'm dangerous." These double standards mirror what Crenshaw (1989) termed "intersectional vulnerability" – the ways in which race, gender, and mental health diagnoses combine to produce unique and intensified forms of marginalisation.

I term this phenomenon "compliant recovery," a coerced, performative healing that privileges institutional legibility over genuine well-being. It is not enough to recover; one must do so visibly, quietly, and on schedule. As a participant put it, "They don't want truth. They want peace and quiet. So, you give them what they want."

But the psychological cost is immense. Internalised surveillance creates a deep emotional alienation. Guilt and shame creep in – about being sectioned, about not being the person others hoped for, about disappointing family. One woman shared, "My mum keeps saying, 'But you were doing so well.' I can't even explain what happened. I just feel like I failed everyone."

As Ahmed (2004) suggests, shame "sticks" to certain bodies more than others, particularly those already racialised and gendered as problematic. In this way, shame is not a private flaw but a public consequence of being positioned as deviant, broken, or insufficiently healed. Shame operates as a technology of control – governing the self by attaching pain to visibility.

This affective management also speaks to hooks (1989), who contends that Black women are taught to feel shame for taking up space, for speaking back, and for existing outside of control. The guilt that follows a breakdown, or a failure to recover on schedule, is not simply personal; it is structural. It reflects the historical expectation that women of colour should be strong, composed, and silent.

Page's (2017) work on institutional betrayal is particularly resonant here. She argues that individuals who are harmed by institutions often carry the shame of that harm as though it were their own fault, especially when the institution frames its neglect as support. One participant noted, "They acted like they saved me. But I'm the one who has to carry what they did."

The performance of recovery often crushes self-esteem. Rather than feeling restored, participants described a gnawing sense of fraudulence, as though the person they were presenting was not quite real, and the risk of being "found out" hovered constantly. Berlant's (2011) concept of "cruel optimism" captures this well: the very promise of recovery becomes its own burden, foreclosing the space for complex or non-linear healing.

This flattening of emotion and identity also echoes Cvetkovich's (2003) framing of trauma as a felt structure. Trauma here is not defined by dramatic events but by the quiet accrual of constrained expression, forced silences, and relational breakdowns. The demand to perform recovery often creates the very harm it claims to resolve.

And yet, refusal exists. Sarcasm, irony, and selective silence become quiet revolts. One woman shared, "I say what they want to hear. Then I play my music and dance when no one's looking." This echoes Lorde's (1984) assertion that survival is a form of resistance, especially when it interrupts scripts of docility.

Ultimately, the performance of recovery is not merely about survival within an ableist system; it is about negotiating dignity within its shadows. It is exhausting. It is strategic. And it is not freedom.

The next section examines the failures of NHS aftercare and the racialised bureaucracy of community mental health systems.

Haunted by harm: The residue of institutional contact

The harm that institutionalisation inflicts does not end with the last ward round. For many, the psychiatric institution leaves a residue rather than a scar. It is thick, enduring, and difficult to name. As Cvetkovich (2003) writes, trauma is often sedimented in the ordinary; it is not always violent or dramatic but is present in what feels suddenly unbearable.

Many participants described avoiding hospitals entirely post-discharge, even for unrelated issues. Others refused to attend GP surgeries, frightened that their concerns would be minimised or reinterpreted through a psychiatric lens. One woman explained, "Even when my chest hurts, I wait. I'd rather suffer at home than be told it's all in my head again."

This anticipatory withdrawal is a product of fear, which Brown (2012) connects with shame and a collapse of trust. But for racialised women, fear is not simply emotional; it is structural. As Ahmed (2004) argues, fear functions as a border patrol, shaping who belongs, who is believable, and who must be watched. The psychiatric label becomes a stain, making every future gesture vulnerable to reinterpretation.

I term this condition "psy-scarred withdrawal," a conscious disengagement from healthcare institutions due to the psychic and social risks of being misread, dismissed, or retraumatised. Participants avoided care not because they rejected help, but because the help they received had harmed them. In this way, institutional betrayal (Smith & Freyd, 2014) continues long after treatment ends.

This lingering fear also reorganises space. One participant said, "I walk the long way just to avoid the hospital. I know it sounds silly, but I panic when I see it." This affective geography, where landscapes themselves trigger embodied reactions, reveals how deeply the institutional experience infiltrates one's sense of safety.

The haunting is not metaphorical. It is mapped onto the body and the built environment. It shows up in the way women hesitate before naming pain, question whether they're "overreacting," or pre-emptively tone down their speech. These are not neuroses; they are strategies of survival in a world that has already decided what they are.

Let's return, then, to the words of Butler (2004): to be recognisable is not always to be safe. For those exiting psychiatric institutions, the condition of being known – as once mad, once broken, once institutionalised – often guarantees exposure, not care. The harm persists, not in spite of the institution but because of its reach.

And yet, in the midst of this residue, women still navigate, adapt, and resist. Their fear is not a weakness; it is a map of what they have endured. Their caution is not paranoia; it is an archive of past violence. And their silence is not emptiness; it is strategy.

In what follows, we turn to the fractured solidarities, the interrupted intimacies, and the quiet acts of reclamation that make up the post-institutional life.

Fractured solidarities and intimate disruptions

Leaving the institution also meant re-entering social worlds that had shifted, or that had shifted away. For many women, institutionalisation ruptured not only health but also relationships. Partners, friends, colleagues, and even faith communities became distant, hesitant, or patronising. One participant put it simply: "People don't know how to be around you after you've been 'in there.'"

This post-institutional estrangement reflects what hooks (2000) describes as the failure of care under patriarchy, where relational labour disproportionately falls on women and where deviation from emotional expectations results in abandonment. Several participants spoke of partners who withdrew, not because of malice but because they lacked the emotional language to stay. "He said I'd changed," one woman said. "But it was the silence between us that had changed me."

Others described fractured kinship, where families imposed silence rather than support. "They said not to talk about it," one woman recalled. "They were embarrassed." Here, silence becomes both a symptom and a tool of oppression, echoing Lorde's (1984) insistence that "your silence will not protect you."

Trust, once broken by institutional betrayal, rarely reassembled easily. Even when loved ones tried, the shadow of medical authority loomed. One woman said her mother would call daily to "check in," but it always felt like surveillance. "It wasn't 'how are you?' It was 'are you taking your meds?'"

This strain on intimacy was not incidental. It was compounded by the racialised burden of appearing stable, grateful, or reformed. As Bhopal (2018) argues, institutional racism is not confined to policies; it saturates interpersonal interactions. Women of colour bore the added weight of disproving the diagnosis, constantly performing recovery to avoid being read as dangerous, broken, or burdensome.

Even more acutely, some women shared that their partners, particularly men, simply left. They withdrew without conversation, sometimes citing confusion and other times offering no explanation at all. For some, the presence of distress was treated as something too inconvenient or uncomfortable to acknowledge, something easier to walk away from than to understand.

Their absence spoke volumes: mental health became a boundary they were unwilling to cross. This reflects what Ahmed (2014) calls "fragile solidarities" – connections that fracture under the pressure of embodied difference. Here, the perceived unpredictability of mental distress was met not with intimacy but with withdrawal.

The psychic wound of this desertion cannot be dismissed. It is shaped by gendered expectations around emotional labour and the myth of the "strong Black woman" – a trope that simultaneously dehumanises and demands resilience. The failure of partners and loved ones to remain present becomes a second institutionalisation: abandonment as repetition of the ward's disconnection.

In the absence of understanding, many turned inward, or towards alternative forms of kinship. Piepzna-Samarasinha (2018) offers the framework of "crip kinship," a model of community built on shared vulnerability and collective care rather than on perfection or performance. Some participants described new friendships formed in support groups, online spaces, or informal networks. "We didn't have to explain everything," one said. "We just knew."

Still, the cost of relational rupture was steep. Isolation, mistrust, and guilt became common themes. Participants mourned not only the people who left but the selves they could no longer be in those relationships. As one woman put it, "It's not just that they didn't show up. It's that I stopped expecting them to."

These fractured solidarities are not private failures, but they are extensions of institutional violence. Psychiatric harm travels; it inhabits bedrooms, text messages, and empty pews. To heal, then, is not just to recover one's health but to reconstruct relational safety.

And even here, the work is uneven.

As one participant put it, "I can forgive the system before I forgive the people I loved who disappeared." This reminds us that while institutional violence is devastating, it is often the silence, absence, or abandonment by loved ones that cuts the deepest. The betrayal by those closest – those expected to stay – can leave wounds that feel more personal and less explainable than systemic harm. It underscores how psychiatric experiences fracture not only the self, but also the relational worlds that surround it.

Slow ethics, small joys: Rebuilding trust in the everyday

For those exiting psychiatric institutions, healing was rarely described as a dramatic transformation. Instead, it unfolded in fragments: planting herbs on the windowsill, making tea without flinching at the kettle's hiss, stepping outside without surveillance. These were not moments of cure, but of *reorientation*, acts that quietly defied the institutional grammar of compliance, fear, and pathology. Recovery, as narrated by participants, was less about symptom removal and more about reinhabiting the ordinary with dignity.

This speaks to what María Puig de la Bellacasa (2017) calls "slow ethics," an ethics of care grounded not in grand interventions but in mundane, relational practices. For the women in this study, healing was not an endpoint but a repeated, contingent act. Hanging out laundry. Laughing at a friend's joke without wondering if it was "allowed." Feeling cold and naming it. These were small but profound gestures of re-worlding.

Slow ethics resists the pace and expectations of biomedical recovery timelines, which often frame healing as linear, measurable, and externally validated. Instead, it centres attentiveness, patience, and the value of the unremarkable. "I had to relearn how to live," said one participant. "Not because I was broken – but because the world had become sharp." Her remark reminds us that the harm was not internal but environmental. Recovery, then, was about softening the world rather than about fixing the self.

This slow return to the self also operated through what Berlant (2011) terms "lateral agency" – the pursuit of small acts of survival and enjoyment that may not be liberatory in the traditional sense but sustain life in oppressive conditions. For some, this meant journaling in the park; for others, it was giving themselves permission to grieve without rushing. "I cried in the bath," one woman said. "Not because I was sad, but because I was allowed."

These small joys were not naive. They emerged against the backdrop of persistent structural violence. But they refused to let institutions be the sole narrators of life after diagnosis. They also created spaces of refusal, where women could assert care on their own terms, outside the logics of therapy, compliance, or psychiatric readability. "I stopped telling my care coordinator how I feel," said one participant. "Now I tell my plants."

Theorists such as Hartman (1997) and Campt (2017) have argued that in spaces where life is constrained, *minor gestures* – those fleeting, quiet refusals – can be radical. In the context of this study, such gestures offered counterpoints to the overwhelming weight of institutional histories. Even acts of non-engagement (ignoring a phone call from a mental health service, choosing not to explain oneself) became strategies for self-preservation.

Importantly, joy itself became political. As Audre Lorde (1984) insists, "Caring for myself is not self-indulgence – it is self-preservation, and that is an act of political warfare." In this frame, joy was not the erasure of pain but the insistence on worth amid it. "I dance every morning," said one woman. "Just a little. Even when I'm tired. It reminds me I'm still here."

The recovery imagined by institutions often demands silence, obedience, and gratitude. The recovery narrated by participants in this study demanded slowness, refusal, and rehumanisation. These small acts of joy and care were not symbols of compliance, but traces of resistance – emblems of a life reassembled, piece by piece, on their own terms.

Conclusion. Beyond discharge: Reclaiming freedom, disrupting scripts

Discharge is not freedom. This chapter has traced how the institutional logic of psychiatry lingers long after the ward has been left: migrating through neighbourhood whispers, GP visits, workplace silences, and even the mirror. The women whose voices ground this work do not speak of recovery as a clean break but as a contested process marked by vigilance, fatigue, and conditional visibility. Their post-discharge lives are not voids; they are battlegrounds where they navigate the burden of becoming legible, compliant, and well-performing subjects.

The transition from patient to "well person" is not merely medical, but also cultural, racialised, and deeply gendered. Institutions teach a choreography of wellness: how to smile without seeming manic, how to speak without sounding erratic, how to dress, answer, and even sigh. This performative burden is intensified for Black and Brown women, whose histories of pathologisation and social abandonment intersect violently with post-institutional expectations. As one participant said, "You recover for them, not for yourself."

What we can see, then, is not failure to reintegrate but the persistence of carceral logic outside the frame of confinement. The ward produces more than psychiatric patients. It produces self-doubting, self-monitoring, strategically compliant citizens trained to fear their own emotions and second-guess their own instincts. What Lauren Berlant would call *cruel optimism* lives here: the idea that performing recovery will eventually lead to freedom, even as the very demand to perform becomes the chain that imprisons.

And yet, resistance pulses through the cracks: in sarcasm, in cultural reclamation, in speaking back to coordinators, in singing to oneself without apology. Survival is not silent. It is improvisational. It is an act of fugitive refusal that refuses to be flattened by clinical categories or institutional scripts.

The question, then, is not only about what happens after discharge but also about what kind of world awaits. If surveillance has no walls, our response must also be without bounds: it has to be radical, relational, and reparative. Aftercare must become *care*, not control. Listening must replace assessment. Belonging must replace pathology.

This chapter does not offer easy solutions. But it has insisted that the afterlife of psychiatric contact is not inevitable. It is political. And it is changeable if we learn to hear survivors as theorists of survival rather than as merely a group of symptoms.

Reflexive questions for the reader

- When you encounter someone who has experienced psychiatric care, what assumptions do you make?
- How do everyday systems – schools, clinics, workplaces – replicate institutional logic?
- Have you ever misread silence, emotion, or cultural expression through a lens of pathology?
- What would care look like if it prioritised listening, solidarity, and co-created meaning?
- How do your own professional or familial roles inadvertently surveil rather than support?

References

Ahmed, S. (2004). *The Cultural Politics of Emotion*. Edinburgh University Press.

Ahmed, S. (2012). *On Being Included: Racism and Diversity in Institutional Life*. Duke University Press.

Ahmed, S. (2014). *Willful subjects*. Durham, NC: Duke University Press.

Berlant, L. (2011). *Cruel Optimism*. Duke University Press.

Ben-Moshe, L. (2020). *Decarcerating Disability: Deinstitutionalization and Prison Abolition*. University of Minnesota Press.

Benjamin, R. (2019). *Race after technology: Abolitionist tools for the New Jim Code*. Cambridge: Polity Press.

Bhopal, K. (2018). *White Privilege: The Myth of a Post-Racial Society*. Policy Press.

Brown, B. (2012). *Daring Greatly*. Gotham Books.

Butler, J. (2004). *Undoing Gender*. Routledge.

Campt, T. M. (2017). *Listening to images*. Durham, NC: Duke University Press.

Collins, P. H. (2000). *Black feminist thought: Knowledge, consciousness, and the politics of empowerment*. 2nd edn. New York: Routledge.

Crenshaw, K. (1989). *Demarginalizing the Intersection of Race and Sex*. University of Chicago Legal Forum.

Cvetkovich, A. (2003). *An Archive of Feelings: Trauma, Sexuality, and Lesbian Public Cultures*. Duke University Press.

Foucault, M. (1997). *Discipline and punish: The birth of the prison*. Translated by A. Sheridan. New York: Vintage Books.

Goffman, E. (1961). *Asylums: Essays on the Social Situation of Mental Patients and Other Inmates*. Anchor Books.

Hartman, S. (1997). *Scenes of subjection: Terror, slavery, and self-making in nineteenth-century America*. New York: Oxford University Press.

hooks, b. (1989). *Talking back: Thinking feminist, thinking Black*. Boston, MA: South End Press.

hooks, b. (2000). *All About Love: New Visions*. William Morrow.

Lorde, A. (1984). *Sister Outsider: Essays and Speeches*. Crossing Press.

Page, T. (2017). 'Vulnerable writing as a feminist methodological practice', *Feminist Review*, 115(1), pp. 13–29.

Piepzna-Samarasinha, L. L. (2018). *Care Work: Dreaming Disability Justice*. Arsenal Pulp Press.

Puig de la Bellacasa, M. (2017). *Matters of care: Speculative ethics in more than human worlds*. Minneapolis and London: University of Minnesota Press.

Rose, N. (1999). *Powers of Freedom: Reframing Political Thought*. Cambridge University Press.

Smith, C. P. and Freyd, J. J. (2014). Institutional betrayal. *American Psychologist*, 69(6), 575–587.

9

What I could not say in the ward Memory, love, rage, and the unspoken truths

Holding silence, naming refusal

Chapter 8 exposed how the institution never fully ends after discharge – how it lingers in bodies, homes, and GP appointments – but this chapter shifts the focus. It centres the unsaid, the edited, and the quietly withheld. We examine what could not be spoken inside the psychiatric ward, not because there was nothing to say, but because saying it had consequences. Here, we move from visible acts of resistance to the subtler realm of epistemic refusal: strategic silence.

This is not a repetition of previous themes, but a deepening of the analysis. While Chapter 7 explored life inside the ward and

Chapter 8 the afterlife of surveillance, Chapter 9 theorises silence itself – silence not as a void but as a practice. Silence not as failure to resist, but as a survival strategy shaped by race, gender, class, and institutional risk. Following Campt (2017), we can read quiet not as absence but as a recalibrated form of dissent. Silence is a tactic. But it is also a wound.

Strategic silence as survival

Participants made calculated decisions to withhold truth, tailor their language, or simplify their stories. These silences were not gaps in memory but acts of strategic communication. As one woman reflected: "I knew better than to say too much. I saw what happened to the girl who mentioned her trauma. They labelled her borderline before she finished her sentence."

This silence becomes a form of risk management. In institutions where disclosure is equated with instability, speaking honestly can lead to punishment or intensified scrutiny. For women of colour, whose words are already filtered through racialised and gendered assumptions, silence often becomes a necessary strategy for survival.

As Collins (2000) describes in her work on controlling images and racialised motherhood, Black women must negotiate a public script that renders them hyper-visible and yet perpetually disbelieved.

One participant recalled: "If I had said how bad it was with my partner, they might have taken my child. I couldn't risk that. So, I said I was fine." This dilemma, where speaking can endanger rather than protect, reflects a politics of containment. It also resonates with Crenshaw's (1991) concept of structural intersectionality where multiple systems of oppression converge to render some forms of pain illegible and therefore unspeakable.

The fear of being too coherent

In institutional psychiatric contexts, the speaking Black woman is not a neutral subject. Her coherence – her ability to articulate experience, critique power, or deploy theoretical language – is not read as capacity but as a threat. Across multiple narratives in this study, participants described the compulsion to perform a diluted version of themselves in order to avoid punitive consequences.

One participant said, "I kept it simple. No big words. You use theory, and they think you're manic." This account captures a central paradox: that clarity of thought rather than signifying recovery or insight is treated with suspicion. As Foucault (1977) theorises, disciplinary institutions maintain power not only through physical constraint but through the regulation of speech and meaning. In this case, linguistic control becomes a proxy for psychiatric order. The act of speaking, particularly with fluency, symbolism, or theoretical reflection, is reframed as pathology.

Participants were acutely aware of this distortion. One woman explained: "They said I sounded rehearsed. That I must have Googled it all. I teach – of course I use language. But when I explained my feelings, they said I was manipulating them." This is not merely anecdotal. It reflects what Medina (2013) terms epistemic *injustice*, whereby individuals from marginalised groups are discredited or dismissed precisely because of their social positioning. In this case, Black women's intellectual capacities are rendered illegible or disallowed within clinical scripts that demand submission, muteness, and infantilisation.

Fanon's (1967) critique of colonial subjectivity further contextualises this misrecognition. The articulate Black subject disrupts the colonial imaginary of the incoherent Other. The very act of naming one's condition – of offering analysis – becomes an insubordinate gesture. In psychiatric space, this tension becomes lethal: women's speech is rewritten as delusion, their clarity documented as danger.

One participant reflected on the aftershock of such reframing: "I made a joke about escaping once – just a joke – and they logged it as 'planning elopement.' After that, I just nodded and smiled." This is not simply individualised fear. It is evidence of institutional codes – what Ahmed (2012) calls *non-performatives* – in which the appearance of listening masks a refusal to hear. Within this framework, the psychiatric institution positions itself as receptive, even benevolent, while structurally foreclosing Black women's narrations of harm.

The result is coerced reduction. Participants described actively deconstructing their own verbal registers, removing metaphor, silencing critique, and softening intonation, all to avoid punitive psychiatric interpretation. This was not submission, but survival: a form of self-regulation enacted under surveillance.

As such, silence was not experienced as failure but as necessary recalibration. The more coherent they were, the more incoherent they were assumed to be. It is not simply that language was policed, but that the very legitimacy of Black women's subjectivity was placed under institutional erasure.

Silence among patients: Isolation and alienation

The psychiatric institution does not merely contain individuals; it strategically fragments relationships. Across participant narratives, a consistent pattern emerged: communication between patients, particularly sustained or intimate communication, was discouraged or directly interrupted by staff. Proximity, even when non-verbal, was read as disorderly.

One participant described this: "We weren't supposed to talk too long. If they saw you together, they'd separate you. They didn't want friendships, only order." This institutional disciplining of relationships aligns closely with Goffman's (1961) formulation of the *total institution*, which seeks to dismantle the individual's former identity by regulating every aspect of their environment, including social interaction. But in the racialised psychiatric context, this control takes on a further dimension: the policing of community among those already structurally silenced.

Participants described how even small gestures of care or camaraderie – offering a listening ear, sitting side by side, or sharing cultural references – were treated as forms of deviance. One woman recounted

> We weren't allowed in each other's rooms. I wanted to check on someone after she was restrained, just sit with her. A nurse saw me and said I was interfering with care.

Such narratives point to an institutional logic that views connection as contamination. Patients, particularly women of colour, were systematically denied access to each other's stories. As Lorde (1984) has argued, "Our silence will not protect us," but within this setting, silence was not simply internal; it was imposed, enforced, and policed.

This tactic serves a double function: it prevents collective witnessing and breaks the possibility of shared truth. In denying women the space to affirm one another's experiences, the institution neutralises their capacity to speak as a "we." The psychiatric gaze thus isolates both physically and epistemologically; it ensures that no single woman can corroborate another's version of harm.

The alienation this produced was deeply felt. One participant remarked: "I needed someone to say, 'Yes, I saw that too.' But we were never left alone long enough." This denial of communal validation created an atmosphere of suspicion and mistrust. When women did manage to speak with one another, they often felt they had to whisper, scan the room for cameras, or keep their bodies turned away from doorways.

One participant said, "We used to write things in the Bibles. That was the only thing they didn't check. I still have some of those pages." Here, resistance emerges not through confrontation but through hidden inscriptions, what hooks (1990) calls "homeplace": the creation of safe spaces within hostile institutions. But even these acts were vulnerable to exposure and subject to interpretation through the lens of institutional paranoia.

In this way, the psychiatric ward operates not only as a space of medical intervention but also as a site of epistemic fragmentation. Solidarity becomes a clinical risk; connection is rewritten as collusion. The very tools of collective survival – testimony, witness, and relationships – are rendered unstable. And in their absence, women begin to question not only the system but also themselves.

Silence after discharge: The lingering gag

The end of inpatient care did not signify the end of silencing. For many participants, discharge marked the beginning of a more insidious form of containment, one in which their attempts to narrate what had happened to them were dismissed, doubted, or pathologised. Silence, in this context, was no longer enforced by ward routines or staff supervision but by the pervasive disbelief of wider society.

One of the women said, "I tried to explain what happened in the ward. The therapist said, 'That sounds like paranoia.' I shut down. I never mentioned it again." This account reflects what Ahmed (2012) conceptualises as *non-performative institutionalism*: the institutional promise to listen or support does not result in meaningful recognition or structural change. Instead, institutions adopt the language of care without doing the work of validation. The consequence is a form of rhetorical gaslighting, where those who speak the truth are met with diagnostic suspicion rather than believed.

Several participants described moments where their memories of psychiatric harm were not treated as evidence but as further symptoms. One woman recalled being told: "You seem to have held on to a lot of resentment. That's not healthy." This medicalised framing of righteous anger, where rage becomes a sign of dysfunction rather than a response to violence, exemplifies what Ahmed (2014) calls *affective discipline*. Emotional responses that challenge the legitimacy of the institution are reframed as personal pathology. The survivor becomes suspect precisely because she remembers too much, too clearly.

Moreover, participants expressed a growing awareness that recounting their experiences in too much detail could jeopardise access to future services. Speaking honestly became a strategic risk. As one participant put it, "I knew if I said too much, they'd put it back in the notes. Then the next person would treat me like a problem, not a person." In this way, the medical file, ostensibly a record of care, becomes a tool of anticipatory control. The institution's power extends beyond physical walls into the language that follows survivors across appointments years after inpatient treatment and relationships.

This echoes Spivak's (1988) foundational argument about the subaltern's capacity to speak: it is not merely about voice, but about the conditions under which speech is legible. In psychiatric aftercare, the terms of legibility are tightly controlled. To critique the institution, even in retrospect, is to risk re-pathologisation. The system protects itself through its diagnostic gaze, ensuring that those who name it as violent are framed as unreliable.

Another participant captured this chilling circularity: "They said, 'Well you seem fine now, so maybe it wasn't that bad.' But when I was in there, they said I was too coherent to be believed. So which is it?" The implication is that Black women are never the right kind of patient; they are too broken to be trusted, too articulate to be believed, too angry to be rational, and too silent to be real. This epistemic tightrope leaves little room for narrative autonomy. As Medina (2013) argues, *testimonial injustice* does not just silence; it rewrites memory, corrodes self-trust, and distorts reality.

For many, the safest option became silence, not because they had nothing to say, but because they had already seen what happened when they tried to speak.

Theorising shame and guilt

Shame and guilt were not incidental after-effects of institutionalisation; they were deliberately structured outcomes of psychiatric control. Across interviews, women described these emotions not merely as personal feelings but as embodied responses to an environment that engineered internal collapse. For example, one participant said: "I kept thinking I had failed everyone. My mum, my daughter, even my community. Like I had broken the image of a strong Black woman."

This aligns with recent scholarship that frames shame as a disciplinary technology (Brown, 2021; Probyn, 2005). Within psychiatric systems, shame is not simply felt; it is cultivated. Institutions deploy rituals of exposure, infantilisation, and restraint to degrade the self, producing a subject who not only obeys but questions her own legitimacy.

Ahmed (2004) describes shame as a "turning inward," a pulling of the body back into itself. Participants echoed this physicality. One woman described not making eye contact for weeks after discharge. Another said: "I didn't even want to walk the same street near the hospital. I thought people could tell. Like I was marked."

For Black women, shame is racialised, gendered, and surveilled. It is intensified by the performance of strength that many have been taught to embody. As Bhopal (2018) argues, the ideal of the "strong Black woman" is not liberatory when it becomes a disciplinary demand. Instead, it sets an impossible standard – one that shifts the blame for institutional failures onto the individual. When support systems collapse, Black women are not seen as failed by the system, but as personally inadequate for not coping well enough. Recent research by Alldred and Fox (2023) emphasises that guilt and shame are used in institutional contexts to produce conformity, not through coercion alone, but through *affective undermining*. These emotions are encouraged subtly: by praising compliance, pathologising resistance, and discouraging expressions of injustice.

Participants noted that guilt often emerged in relation to others: guilt because they had been discharged while others had not, guilt for speaking out, or guilt for no longer feeling unwell. One woman said: "I felt bad for getting better. I felt like I'd abandoned the others who helped me survive in there." This is what Lugones (2003) might call a "loving guilt," a guilt born from relationality, not wrongdoing. But psychiatry does not read guilt this way. Instead, such emotions are folded back into diagnosis, further entrenching women in a cycle where survival becomes suspect and healing is never neutral.

Ahmed (2010) helps us understand this dynamic through the concept of "affective economies": the circulation of feelings across bodies and spaces. In the psychiatric setting, guilt and shame are not individual flaws. They are tools of regulation that are circulated between patients and staff and reinforced through observation, notes, and silences. They do not end at discharge; they follow survivors into everyday life, shaping how they speak, trust, and relate. One participant, for example, said, "Even after I got out, I stopped talking about what happened. Not because I'd healed – but because every time I tried, I felt like I was doing something wrong." This is the end goal of psychiatric shame: not rehabilitation, but withdrawal. A retreat from voice, from resistance, from connection, and crucially, from truth-telling.

When Black and racialised women begin to see themselves not as failed but as forcibly fractured, that is, when they name shame and guilt as structural weapons, they begin to unlearn the lie that their silence is a personal flaw. It is not. It is evidence of their clarity.

Quiet as recalibrated resistance

Silence, in many psychiatric settings, is constructed as pathology. A quiet patient may be read as withdrawn, unresponsive, or emotionally disengaged. Yet, within the narratives of the women in this study, silence was not always the absence of voice. It was often a tactic, a form of resistance shaped by survival.

One woman said, "Sometimes I pretended I didn't understand. It bought me time. I didn't have to answer straight away." This form of self-preservation reflects what Ortega (2006) conceptualises as home tactics – the small, often unnoticed strategies of survival that racialised women use to navigate spaces that render them hyper-visible and disposable. These tactics are not necessarily loud, confrontational, or explicitly oppositional. They are embodied manoeuvres that allow women to retain fragments of agency in the otherwise coercive environments.

Some women learned to speak in ways that would not draw attention. Others learned *not* to speak at all. They whispered through walls, wrote notes in Bibles, or feigned confusion to delay confrontation. Silence, then, was not compliance. It was *delay*, *redirection*, and *slow refusal*.

This recalls Lugones's (2003) notion of *playfulness*, or what she also terms *world-travelling*: the capacity of marginalised subjects, particularly women of colour, to shift between logics and perform roles tactically. When placed in psychiatric systems that read assertiveness as aggression and clarity as delusion, silence became one of the few tools women could wield on their own terms.

"They wanted me to explain why I was upset, but every time I did, they said I was overreacting. So, I stopped. I just nodded and smiled." Here, silence is not passive. It is a calculated disengagement from systems that do not recognise or honour the speaker. This aligns with Moten and Harney's (2013) idea of the *fugitive practice*: a refusal to perform the legible scripts expected by the institution, even if that refusal looks like withdrawal.

However, this tactic was not without consequences. Women spoke of the cruel reversals they experienced once discharged: those who had learned to survive through quietness were now disbelieved precisely *because* of their coherence. Their pain was reinterpreted through retrospective scepticism.

> People would say things like, "Ah, so you remember what happened – then you weren't really crazy." Or, "You weren't yourself back then," when I tried to explain how I was treated. Like my version of events couldn't be trusted.

This reveals a structural bind. Inside the institution, silence is interpreted as lack of insight' and outside of it, speech is viewed as evidence that no harm occurred. This is what Medina (2013) identifies as *epistemic injustice*, the systemic undermining of one's credibility as a knower, particularly when one's knowledge disrupts dominant narratives.

In this light, even silence after discharge can be read as a continued survival strategy. One participant explained: "I started writing things down instead of saying them out loud. Just for me. It was safer that way." This shift, from public speech to private documentation, can be seen as a form of what Hartman (2008) might call *critical fabulation*: a refusal to offer trauma as spectacle, paired with a determination to narrate on one's own terms. Silence, in this sense, becomes not the absence of voice but the reclamation of narrative autonomy.

Yet this strategy is precarious. When silence is framed solely as dysfunction, its tactical dimensions are erased. When women of colour choose silence, they are often cast as withholding, suspicious, or emotionally unavailable, reinforcing a cycle where their resistance is reabsorbed into the logic of pathology.

What emerges, then, is a contradictory politics of legibility. Women are expected to speak in ways that confirm institutional truth, but when they speak otherwise, or when they remain silent as a form of critique, their voice is rendered unintelligible. As one participant observed: "No matter what you do, they twist it. You speak, you're manic. You're quiet, you're depressed. There's no way to win."

This impossible calculus shows how racialised women in psychiatry navigate what Crenshaw (1991) describes as *intersectional vulnerability*: the condition of being punished not just for who you are but for how you survive.

To name silence as recalibrated resistance is not to romanticise it. It is to *reclaim* it. To understand it as a response to systems that have long refused to listen. It is to say: silence is not evidence of absence, it is evidence of clarity, of knowing what spaces will do with your truth and choosing not to give it to them.

Conclusion: Refusing the demand to perform pain

This chapter has resituated silence as a politically and affectively charged terrain and not as a passive state; that terrain is crafted in response to structural violence, epistemic policing, and racialised surveillance. For the women whose voices have centred, silence was not simply the absence of speech. It was strategy, shame, wound, and wisdom. It was born of necessity in environments that demanded performance, extracted trauma, and pathologised complexity.

In psychiatric institutions, and in the women's afterlives, silence became both a survival tactic and a form of critique. What could not be said was not necessarily unknown; it was made unspeakable by the risk of disbelief, punishment, or further confinement. In this way, silence is not a sign of incoherence or confusion. It is a deliberate refusal to translate one's pain into the language the institution finds acceptable or legible. It exposes the harsh reality that within the psychiatric systems, being recognised as a "good" or compliant patient often requires performing distress in ways that erase its complexity. Silence, then, becomes a form of resistance, a way of rejecting the unlivable conditions imposed by what some scholars call psychiatric citizenship.

When a woman of colour withholds her story, it is not always because she lacks one. It may be because she knows that, viscerally, her truth will not be believed or worse – that it will be reinterpreted as evidence of instability. This is the machinery of epistemic injustice in action: it not only discredits speech but also pre-empts and disciplines it before it is even uttered.

To treat silence as merely a clinical warning sign is to miss its social and political dimensions. Instead, we must recognise what Tuck and Yang (2014) describe as the "refusal of damage narratives," a deliberate pushback against the coercive invitation to perform victimhood in ways that fit dominant frameworks. Refusal is not a lack. It is a form of integrity.

Yet this refusal is costly. It often comes with guilt, shame, and the loneliness of being unintelligible to systems that demand legibility. Women internalise the watcher, censor their pain, and apologise for their needs. As Lugones (2003) and Ortega (2006) remind us, these are not signs of submission but of tactical navigation, of life lived at the borderlands of sense and power.

And so, this chapter does not end with a call to "break the silence" in the conventional sense. Instead, it invites a different practice of listening – one that can hold silence without demanding its conversion into confession. One that does not equate wellness with speech, or pathology with withholding. One that understands silence as both a symptom of institutional betrayal and a strategy for survival within it.

This is not just about psychiatry. It is about what kind of world we want to build. A world where women of colour do not have to trade truth for safety. A world where refusal is legible, silence is respected, and care does not come with the price of extraction.

In the next chapter, "Building Otherwise," we begin that work.

Reflexive questions

1. What assumptions do we carry about silence in clinical spaces, and who benefits when silence is treated as pathology?
2. How might we create spaces where stories of psychiatric harm can be spoken without fear of disbelief, punishment, or institutional revision?
3. In what ways do race, gender, and class shape which forms of speech are heard as credible and which are dismissed as delusion?
4. How can silence be read as refusal rather than failure, and what does this demand from practitioners, allies, and theorists alike?
5. What kind of psychiatric care becomes possible when we stop equating visibility with truth and begin attending to the politics of what is left unsaid?

References

Ahmed, S. (2004). *The Cultural Politics of Emotion*. Edinburgh University Press.

Ahmed, S. (2010). *The promise of happiness*. Durham, NC: Duke University Press.

Ahmed, S. (2012). *On Being Included: Racism and Diversity in Institutional Life*. Duke University Press.

Ahmed, S. (2014). *Willful subjects*. Durham, NC: Duke University Press.

Alldred, P. and Fox, N. J. (2023). 'Applied research, diffractive methodology, and the research-assemblage: Challenges and opportunities', *Sociological Research Online*, 28(1), pp. 93–109.

Bhopal, K. (2018). *White privilege: The myth of a post-racial society.* Bristol: Policy Press.

Brown, A. M. (2021). *Holding change: The way of emergent strategy facilitation and mediation.* Chico, CA: AK Press.

Campt, T. M. (2017). *Listening to Images.* Duke University Press.

Collins, P.H. (2000). *Black Feminist Thought: Knowledge, Consciousness, and the Politics of Empowerment.* 2nd edn. Routledge.

Crenshaw, K. (1991). Mapping the margins: Intersectionality, identity politics, and violence against women of color. *Stanford Law Review,* 43(6), 1241–1299.

Fanon, F. (1967). *Black skin, white masks.* Translated by C. L. Markmann. New York: Grove Press.

Foucault, M. (1977). *Discipline and Punish: The Birth of the Prison.* Penguin.

Goffman, E. (1961). *Asylums: Essays on the Social Situation of Mental Patients and Other Inmates.* Penguin.

Hartman, S. (2008). *Lose your mother: A journey along the Atlantic slave route.* New York: Farrar, Straus and Giroux.

Hooks, b. (1990). *Yearning: Race, gender, and cultural politics.* Boston: South End Press.

Lorde, A. (1984). *Sister Outsider: Essays and Speeches.* Crossing Press.

Lugones, M. (2003). *Pilgrimages/Peregrinajes: Theorizing Coalition Against Multiple Oppressions.* Rowman & Littlefield.

Medina, J. (2013). *The Epistemology of Resistance: Gender and Racial Oppression, Epistemic Injustice, and the Social Imagination.* Oxford University Press.

Moten, F. and Harney, S. (2013). *The undercommons: Fugitive planning & black study.* Wivenhoe, New York, and Port Watson: Minor Compositions.

Ortega, M. (2006). Being lovingly, knowingly ignorant: White feminism and women of color. *Hypatia*, 21(3), 56–74.

Probyn, E. (2005). *Blush: Faces of shame*. Minneapolis: University of Minnesota Press.

Tuck, E. and Yang, K. W. (2014). 'R-words: Refusing research', in Paris, D. and Winn, M. T. (eds.) *Humanizing research: Decolonizing qualitative inquiry with youth and communities*. Thousand Oaks, CA: SAGE, pp. 223–248.

10

Building otherwise: CARE: A decolonial framework for abolitionist mental health

Imagining structural alternatives

Mental health systems in the UK operate as biopolitical laboratories where diagnostic technologies and treatment practices manage the boundaries of legible life. Drawing on Foucault's (1977) theory of biopower, psychiatric institutions become sites where the state regulates populations by delineating whose lives are worth living. Yet, in the case of Black and racialised communities, this biopolitical terrain slips into necropolitics what Mbembe (2003) describes as the state's power to dictate who may live and who must die. In this chapter, I argue that Section 2 of the Mental Health Act 1983 functions as a necropolitical technology: it disproportionately targets Black individuals for involuntary psychiatric detainment, enacting racialised violence under the guise of therapeutic intervention.

Grounded in five years of PAR with psychiatric survivors across the UK, this chapter explores how Section 2 enables state-sanctioned abandonment. Survivors' testimonies – collected through testimonial circles, sousveillance methods, and co-dreamed futures – illuminate how psychiatric institutions codify grief, resistance, and dissent as symptoms of pathology. In doing so, these institutions participate in what Wynter (2003) terms "epistemic violence" where they erase the knowledge and lived realities of those marked as being outside the Western canon of rational, liberal subjecthood.

This chapter adopts Spillers's (1987) theorisation of flesh – that which resists social legibility yet bears the marks of captivity – to centre the affective, political, and ontological violations inflicted through psychiatric carcerality. Rather than seeking minor policy reforms or advocating for the inclusion of marginalised people, such as women of colour, within dominant biomedical frameworks, this argument centres abolitionist epistemologies. These epistemologies reject carceral humanism (Roberts, 2022) and instead imagine relational infrastructures of care that do not rely on surveillance, coercion, or institutional containment. Following Harney and Moten's (2013) notion of *fugitive planning*, the work aims to prefigure insurgent practices that disassemble psychiatry's afterlife.

This chapter proceeds in five parts. The next section maps the global circuits of psychiatric carcerality, situating UK's Section 2 within broader colonial geographies of racialised crisis governance. Section II offers an anatomical critique of the legal, clinical, and epistemic logic embedded in Section 2, arguing that it constitutes both epistemicide and state-sanctioned torture. Section III introduces CARE, a decolonial framework for mental health justice anchored in community-accountable relational ecologies. Section IV surveys prefigurative insurgencies: legislative, spatial, and economic resistances that are already under way. Finally, Section V reflects on the methodology of resistance enacted by survivors themselves; their epistemologies materialise alternatives to psychiatric violence.

Global circuits of carcerality: Coloniality in crisis "care"

The limits of Eurocentric reform

In recent years, Northern European models, such as Finland's Open Dialogue, have been promoted as evidence-based alternatives to coercive psychiatry. While these models demonstrate promise in reducing hospitalisation and pharmacological dependency, they often universalise white European subjectivities and fail to grapple with *racialised distress economies* (Ramstead et al., 2022). These economies are shaped by border regimes, austerity, and intergenerational trauma. In the UK, Section 2 of the Mental Health Act 1983 exemplifies what Ruth Wilson Gilmore (2007) terms *organised abandonment*: the systematic neglect of marginalised communities under neoliberal governance.

This abandonment is empirically evident. Black Britons comprise just 3% of the population yet account for 21% of all detentions under Section 2 (NHS Digital, 2022). Moreover, 92% of applications for Section 2 in racialised neighbourhoods are initiated by police officers, not clinicians (Care Quality Commission, 2021). Such data reflect Mills's (2014) critique of *diagnostic imperialism*: the colonial extension of Eurocentric psychiatric categories onto contexts of racial resistance, grief, and survival. As one survivor-researcher, T.O., from the Survivors' Voices

Collective noted: "They called my anger 'mania' – but it was grief for my brother killed in custody."

Global southern epistemologies as abolitionist blueprints

Across the Global South, mental health infrastructures are being radically reimagined, not as sites of biomedical correction but as spaces of community-led repair and resistance. These are not minor reforms. They are abolitionist blueprints: frameworks that reject colonial psychiatry's underlying logic and instead centre relationality, autonomy, and epistemologies of the oppressed.

In Brazil, the *Centros de Atenção Psicossocial* (CAPS) draw on the legacies of *quilombos* – Afro-Brazilian communities founded by escaped enslaved people – as models of collective self-governance. Instead of a system of coercive hospitalisation, care is coordinated through *rodas de conversa* (dialogue circles), where users, carers, and professionals co-design support. These dialogic practices are grounded in mutuality, not in surveillance. Evaluations show that in regions covered by CAPS, hospitalisations have dropped by 73% (Souza, 2021), not because suffering has vanished but because the infrastructure that aims to respond to it has shifted.

South Africa offers another abolitionist grammar through the Ubuntu Respites developed by the Ikhaya Lethu collective. These are not institutions; they are sanctuaries. Guided by the principle of *Ubuntu* – "I am because we are" – healing is structured around relational belonging rather than diagnosis. As one participant shared, "Healing began when they asked, 'Who is waiting for you?' not 'What is your diagnosis?'" This reframing undoes the logic of isolation and reinserts care within a matrix of connection.

Although community organisations like Sangath have made important contributions to peer-led mental health care, their frameworks rarely centre caste. Drawing on Rege's (2003) Dalit feminist epistemologies, one could envisage "vaada" sessions gatherings that locate distress within caste violence, patriarchy, and economic exclusion as a vital corrective, shifting the lens from pathology to structural harm. Here, speaking of pain becomes a political act, a refusal of casteist silencing.

What unites these models is not geography but methodology. They are structured around refusal – the refusal to treat suffering as a defect, the refusal to isolate individuals from their social worlds, and the refusal to use care as a mask for control. Rather than replicating the carceral psychiatric state, these Global Southern approaches build from the ground up, privileging survival knowledge, community sovereignty, and collective futurity.

These are not alternatives. They are indictments. They show us that what exists in the UK is not inevitable; it is chosen. And what is chosen can be dismantled.

Epistemicide and state-sanctioned torture

Anatomising structural violence

Section 2 of the UK's Mental Health Act authorises the involuntary detention of individuals for up to 28 days, often based on ambiguous assessments of "risk." While framed as a protective measure, its application functions less as care and more as carceral intervention, one that disproportionately targets racialised women under the guise of psychiatric necessity.

This legal mechanism enacts what Fanon (1961) terms sociogeny: the pathologisation of Black emotional life as inherently unstable, irrational, or dangerous. The figures speak for themselves. According to NHS Digital (2022), Black Caribbean women are 287% more likely to be detained under Section 2 than white women. Between 2019 and 2023, at least 42 deaths have been officially documented during or shortly after Section 2 detention, numbers that are likely under-reported and insufficiently investigated.

Behind each statistic lies a story of medicalised containment. Women in our interviews shared experiences of being institutionalised after traumatic events – infant loss, racist abuse at work, domestic violence – only to have their grief reinterpreted as "delusional," their dissent marked as "aggression," and their attempts to speak as symptoms of paranoia. In these moments, psychiatry ceases to be therapeutic. It becomes a language of state-sanctioned discipline, what Roberts (2022) terms *carceral humanism*: the weaponisation of care to legitimise punishment.

One woman described being admitted after refusing to leave a GP's office until someone addressed her panic attacks. Another shared how reporting racial bullying at work led to a welfare check – and from there, to a ward. Their distress was real, but its meaning was stolen and replaced with diagnostic shorthand. *Paranoia. Borderline traits. Lacking insight*. These labels travel ahead of the individual, determining how they are spoken to, treated, and surveilled.

This process is not incidental; it is systemic. What we are witnessing is a form of epistemicide: the institutional killing of ways of knowing that do not align with dominant, often white, biomedical frameworks. The Black woman's grief becomes pathology. Her resistance becomes a symptom. Her memory becomes unreliable. And the institution becomes the only legitimate narrator of her experience.

Within this logic, Section 2 is not a neutral holding space. It is a threshold – one that, once crossed, rewrites the subject entirely. It codifies vulnerability as volatility. It turns emotional pain into evidence. And it denies the political roots of distress by individualising its expression.

This is torture in bureaucratic form. It does not rely on overt brutality but on the slow suffocation of autonomy: documentation without consent, medication without explanation, confinement without recourse. And like all systems of racial governance, it is self-justifying. The more the patient resists, the more the system insists it is needed.

These women's stories make clear that Section 2 is not merely misused; it is functioning exactly as designed: to isolate, neutralise, and discredit those whose presence threatens the normative order of psychiatric care. Black women who speak too loudly, ask too many questions, or simply refuse to disappear are rendered *detainable*. Not for their safety, but for institutional peace.

To call this care is to lie.

To challenge it is not simply to ask for reform; it is to demand abolition.

Abolition as a legal and ethical imperative

International scrutiny of the UK's psychiatric regime has intensified in recent years. In 2023, the United Nations Committee on the Rights of Persons with Disabilities concluded that Section 2 of the UK Mental Health Act constitutes a violation of Article 15, which prohibits torture and cruel, inhuman, or degrading treatment. The European Court of Human Rights, in *ZH v Hungary* (2023), similarly held that coercive psychiatric treatment contravenes Article 3, which reinforces the right to dignity and freedom from degrading practices. These legal critiques confirm what racialised survivors have long maintained: that coercive psychiatry is not merely a clinical system with unintended excesses, but a violent apparatus legitimised by law.

Against this backdrop, three immediate demands emerge as both legal and ethical imperatives: first, the repeal of Section 2 and associated detention clauses; second, the redirection of the £1.3 billion allocated annually to psychiatric detainment toward peer-led crisis respites and community-based infrastructures; and third, the statutory enshrinement of the right to refuse treatment, as articulated in the UN Convention on the Rights of Persons with Disabilities (CRPD). These demands are not reformist gestures. They constitute a fundamental repositioning of what it means to respond to distress – one that refuses carcerality as its starting point.

It is within this context that I introduce CARE: a decolonial framework for relational liberation, developed through years of participatory research, survivor-led organising, and theoretical engagement with abolitionist, Black feminist, and Indigenous thought. CARE is not offered as a clinical tool, nor as a codified set of interventions. Rather, it is a counter-infrastructure – a conceptual and material refusal of psychiatry's dominance that is grounded in the lived knowledge of those subjected to it. As an acronym, CARE articulates four interdependent commitments: Community, Accountability, Relationality, and Ecology. Together, they trace a radical alternative to coercive mental health systems, one that foregrounds collective autonomy, reparative justice, and interdependent healing.

Community: Spatial justice as counter-geography

The foundational premise of CARE begins with space. Psychiatric infrastructures often operate through spatial enclosure: the ward, the locked door, the institutional perimeter. Drawing on Massey's (2005) theorisation of space as relational rather than fixed, CARE foregrounds spatial justice as a form of counter-geography. It advocates for the reclamation of space, not simply as physical territory but as relational territory denied by systems of institutional control.

In practice, this could include survivor-led and community-based initiatives that imagine care outside the NHS, beyond the statutory confines of the Mental Health Act — for instance, peer-run crisis sanctuaries, mutual aid circles, communal kitchens, and drop-in spaces that resist the surveillance architecture of formal care. These possibilities, though rarely realised within the UK's tightly regulated framework, point to what care could look like when disentangled from clinical oversight and the perpetual threat of re-admission. For many, even so-called community placements remain tethered to institutional control — some are granted Section 17[1] leave but are never truly free from the shackles of surveillance and the fear of being taken back. Such projects represent spatial refusals: deliberate rejections of institutional spaces that isolate and pathologise. Instead, they insist on care that is communal, embodied, and culturally grounded."Accountability: Refusal as reparative praxis

Within dominant psychiatric logic, accountability is institutional; it is measured through policy reviews, risk audits, and internal inquiries. CARE rejects this bureaucratic framing. Informed by Tuck and K. Yang's (2014) concept of refusal as generative rather than passive, CARE redefines accountability as *reparative praxis*, a mode of action rooted in survivor authority and structural redirection.

Material practices include lived experience councils with binding authority over funding, service design, and policy vetoes; community-led reparative audits to investigate harm; and truth-telling tribunals that mirror transitional justice models, centring survivor testimony as epistemologically and politically authoritative. Refusal, in this context, is not absence but assertion: the capacity to set terms, define harm, and reject institutional mediation. As one participant put it, "Accountability isn't paperwork. It's what happens when survivors don't have to beg for it." Her words sharpen the argument: true accountability cannot be outsourced

1 *Under Section 17 of the Mental Health Act 1983 (as amended 2007), a person detained in hospital for treatment may be granted leave of absence by the responsible clinician. While on Section 17 leave, the individual remains legally detained and can be recalled to hospital at any time. This means that, despite being in the community, the person is still under compulsory powers and not fully discharged from detention.*

to forms or audits. It must be felt, relational, and responsive to those most harmed, not performed through bureaucratic rituals, but embodied in structural change.

Relationality: World-travelling and multiplicity

Conventional psychiatric paradigms discipline individuals into coherence: patients are expected to articulate their pain in recognisable terms, conform to diagnostic scripts, and become legible to clinical authority. CARE, drawing from Lugones's (2003) concept of world-travelling, refuses this demand for coherence. It instead advocates for *relational multiplicity*, wherein care begins with presence, not legibility – with being alongside rather than intervening upon.

In practical terms, this includes retraining practitioners through survivor-led pedagogy; replacing diagnostic intake with listening protocols that ask, "What does this pain ask of us?"; and conducting cultural safety audits that centre racialised and gendered knowledge systems. This approach does not seek to fix the individual but to hold complexity in relational space. As one participant described, "They saw my fear as a symptom – I needed them to see it as a story." Her words speak to a wider demand: that care systems move beyond clinical interpretation and begin to honour the meaning within distress, not simply manage its visibility.

Ecology: Mental health in context

Mainstream psychiatry isolates mental health from broader ecological realities, treating distress as intrapsychic rather than relational or structural. CARE, by contrast, returns mental health to its environmental, historical, and material contexts. Inspired by Whyte's (2018) framing of ecological justice as Indigenous futurity, this dimension insists that dispossession, climate-related grief, food precarity, and urban neglect are not peripheral to distress; they are constitutive of it.

These practices emerge from spaces long marked by exclusion and control – what some refer to as *psychiatric land*: sites once used for confinement and surveillance, now being reclaimed for collective healing. This includes the creation of urban farms on former psychiatric hospital grounds, reconnecting communities with land, rhythm, and seasonal time. It includes climate grief circles led by racialised facilitators, offering space to process intergenerational loss shaped by both colonial extraction and contemporary crisis. And it includes public mourning infrastructures – altars, story walks, and rituals for the disappeared – that honour grief in ways psychiatry has often pathologised or silenced. As one participant put it, "They call it depression. We call it aftershock – from lands we lost, from air we can't breathe."

These practices do more than offer alternative care; they expose the structural conditions that psychiatry too often renders private, individual, or ahistorical. In reclaiming space, story, and ceremony, they shift the terrain of what healing can look like and who gets to define it.

CARE does not propose neutrality. It refuses the premise that psychiatric violence can be rehabilitated through institutional inclusion or cultural competence. Instead, it insists that abolitionist healing already exists – in gardens, kitchens, living rooms, and gatherings where survivors have long theorised care on their own terms. As both a framework and a lived ethic, CARE invites us not to tinker with the machinery of harm but to step outside it entirely.

Summary framing

CARE is not additive to existing services; it is subtractive of state control and multiplicative of survivor power. It refuses the language of inclusion, opting instead for insurgent repair. Its pillars are not steps but entanglements that are co-constituted, iterative, and alive.

Prefigurative insurgencies: Enacting the otherwise

This section traces how abolitionist movements in the Global North and Global South enact the "otherwise" in the present tense, refusing to wait for institutional permission to build liberatory infrastructures. These *prefigurative insurgencies* do not simply critique existing systems, they materially and symbolically anticipate futures beyond coercive psychiatry. In doing so, they foreground the strategic interplay between legal reform, spatial reclamation, and economic redirection.

1. Legislative Jujitsu: Legal Timeframes for Dismantling Carceral Psychiatry

   Drawing inspiration from Brazil's *Lei 10.216/2001* – a landmark law mandating the closure of psychiatric hospitals in favour of community-based care – this model advocates for a binding legal deadline to phase out psychiatric detention in the UK by 2028. Rather than incrementally reforming mental health law, this approach retools the legislative apparatus to accelerate deinstitutionalisation and redirect state funding to survivor-led care collectives. Legal precedent here functions not as compliance but as confrontation – what some scholars term "legislative jujitsu," wherein the law is used tactically to delegitimise the carceral logic it once upheld.

2. Spatial Reclamation: The Localism Act as Terrain for Resistance

 Under the UK Government's *Localism Act 2011*, community groups have statutory rights to reclaim disused public assets, including closed psychiatric wards. Activists and survivor-organisers have begun leveraging this mechanism to occupy and transform former institutional sites into healing justice centres. These spaces not only resist erasure but reframe land itself as a site of care, memory, and reparation. Reclamation here becomes both a material act and a symbolic rupture, repurposing the very architecture of confinement into spaces of relational autonomy.

3. Economic Warfare: Defunding Psychiatry to Fund Survivorship

 Inspired by th e logics of the #DefundPolice movement, survivor-led campaigns have begun targeting NHS mental health budgets as a site of economic redress. By tracing the fiscal flow of psychiatric carcerality – detention, sedation, and surveillance – activists argue for the redirection of these funds into reparative infrastructures, including crisis collectives, grief circles, housing cooperatives, and ecological restoration projects. Economic disinvestment from psychiatry becomes a mode of resistance: a deliberate interruption of the financial lifeblood that sustains coercion under the guise of care.

As outlined in the Introduction, this work is rooted in five years of PAR shaped by methodologies of refusal. In collaboration with psychiatric survivors, abolitionist organisers, and care workers, my approach rejected extractive inquiry in favour of co-theorising, sousveillance, and mutual accountability. These methods, including testimonial circles and dream mapping, are not recounted here in full but are enacted throughout this chapter as insurgent epistemologies. They do not surface as tools of data collection but as practices of relational resistance and survival-based knowledge production.

Abolitionist strategies from the frontlines

Below is a non-exhaustive table of abolitionist strategies used by psychiatric survivors and accomplices that draws inspiration from global and local resistances. These are not policy recommendations but fragments of fugitive planning, practices that signal life beyond Section 2 and psychiatric carcerality.

Strategy	Global inspiration	UK application
Legislative hijack	Brazil's *Conselho Nacional de Saúde* (National Health Council), where service users help steer health policy.	Amend the NHS Constitution to include binding veto power for survivor councils over involuntary treatment frameworks.

Strategy	Global inspiration	UK application
Spatial occupation	Disability justice activists occupying San Francisco's Health and Human Services building (504 Sit-In, 1977).	Reclaim disused psychiatric wards or local clinics as community-run healing spaces governed by service users.
Care mutualism	Black Panthers' Free Clinics and Mutual Aid networks.	Expand survivor-led peer support networks and crisis sanctuaries decoupled from police or NHS referral pathways.
Archival subversion	The ACT UP Oral History Project documenting the HIV/AIDS crisis from below.	Build encrypted survivor-led repositories of testimony and evidence detailing abuses under Section 2.
De-medicalised crisis response	CAHOOTS (Crisis Assistance Helping Out On The Streets), Eugene, Oregon.	Fund survivor- and community-led mobile mental health teams independent of police and trained in non-pathologising care.

Strategy	Global inspiration	UK application
Anti-psych surveillance (Sousveillance)	Indigenous Land Defenders using GoPros and encrypted comms to monitor the RCMP (Royal Canadian Mounted Police) in Canada.	Use encrypted documentation (audio, video, texts) to record detainments, coercion, and restraint incidents under Sections 2 and 35.
Creative refusal	South African shack dwellers' movement (Abahlali baseMjondolo [The Residents of the Shacks]) using art, poetry, and music as political tools.	Foster survivor-led theatre, poetry slams, and zine-making collectives to challenge dominant psychiatric narratives.
Kinship as infrastructure	Queer and disabled kinship networks in Puerto Rico post-Hurricane Maria.	Build solidarity housing, transport-sharing systems, and care webs to reduce dependency on institutional services.

These strategies are not blueprints, but openings. They embody a refusal to negotiate with systems built on extraction, incarceration, and epistemic violence. They suggest that abolition is not just about closing psychiatric hospitals, it is also about decolonising care, reimagining health, and centring those who have always been deemed disposable.

In the end, survivors do not seek to be folded gently back into the system. Many do not want better cages or more comfortable sedation. They want the world to be otherwise. And in the echoes of Section 2's wards, in the trembling but steady voices of those who survived them, we hear not just pain but prophecy.

Conclusion: Fugitive horizons

The dismantling of Section 2 is not merely a juridical imperative; it is a generative rupture in the architecture of psychiatric carcerality. It marks the possibility of refusing coercion as care, and it opens space for alternative modes of living, relating, and healing. As this chapter argues, CARE is not a technocratic model or a reformist addendum to existing policy. It is a fugitive infrastructure, a relational blueprint built outside and against the logic of institutional control.

Rooted in abolitionist praxis and Black feminist thought, CARE insists that survivors are not passive recipients of intervention but theorists of freedom: they are archivists of refusal and planners of what Gilmore (2022, p.231) calls "the rehearsal for life." To abolish Section 2 is to assert that no one is disposable. It is to reclaim the right to be cared for without captivity, to grieve without surveillance, and to be in pain without being pathologised.

As Cabello (2024) reminds us: "Our trembles are compasses pointing home, not pathologies to be silenced." This is not metaphorical. It is a radical reorientation of what constitutes knowledge, care, and futurity. Survivors do not require institutional validation to know what healing feels like. What they require is space to enact it. What they require is resourcing, not regulation. What they require is an end to forced treatment disguised as protection.

The world that abolition builds is not born from tinkering with policy or making philanthropic gestures. It emerges through fugitive planning, relational insurgency, and the practice of radical love. These are not utopian abstractions. They are the daily, embodied labours of those who survive systems designed to disappear them.

The revolution begins not with institutional approval but when survivor silence is recognised as epistemology. When trembling becomes testimony. When refusal becomes repair.

Reflexive questions for the chapter

> I believe to write from the wound is not to seek sympathy.
> It is to demand that knowledge be made accountable.

The questions that follow are rooted in that belief. They also guided the writing of this chapter, anchoring it in a politics of refusal, relational accountability, and epistemic integrity:

1. Whose knowledge is being centred, and who remains illegible?
    - How does this chapter interrupt psychiatric and academic tendencies to invalidate survivor knowledge, especially that of Black, disabled, and racialised individuals?
2. What violences are reproduced in the act of writing about violence?
    - How do I name institutional harm without reinscribing trauma, voyeurism, or spectacle?
    - What ethical lines do I draw when quoting survivor testimony?

3. What do I refuse, and why?
   - Why does this chapter reject reformist discourse, biomedical validation, and institutional neutrality?
   - How do those refusals act as care, not obstruction?
4. What is my proximity to the systems I critique, and how do I remain accountable?
   - As a researcher, survivor, or ally, where do I benefit from or resist the psychiatric state?
   - How is accountability enacted *beyond* citation?
5. What world does this chapter imagine, and who is it for?
   - Does this work offer a path towards abolitionist care, or does it merely critique?
   - Who can use this chapter as a tool, a mirror, or a map?

These questions are not designed to resolve discomfort. They are a method of staying close to it – of writing not *about* survivors but *with* and *towards* them in pursuit of justice that refuses to negotiate with carcerality.

References

Cabello, M. (2024). *Science and religious dogmatism*. Available at: https://papers.ssrn.com/sol3/papers.cfm?abstract_id=4972195 (Accessed: 28 September 2025).

Care Quality Commission (2021). *Monitoring the Mental Health Act in 2020/21*. London: CQC. Available at: https://www.cqc.org.uk/publications/monitoring-mental-health-act-2020-21

European Court of Human Rights (2023). *ZH v. Hungary*, Application no. 28973/16, Judgment of 19 January 2023. Available at: https://hudoc.echr.coe.int/eng?i=001-221965 (Accessed: 28 September 2025).

Fanon, F. (1961). *The wretched of the earth*. Translated by C. Farrington. New York: Grove Press.

Foucault, M. (1977). *Discipline and Punish: The Birth of the Prison*. Translated by A. Sheridan. London: Penguin.

Gilmore, R. W. (2007). *Golden Gulag: Prisons, surplus, crisis, and opposition in globalizing California*. Berkeley: University of California Press.

Gilmore, R. W. (2022). *Abolition geography: Essays towards liberation*. London: Verso.

Harney, S. and Moten, F. (2013). *The Undercommons: Fugitive Planning and Black Study*. New York: Minor Compositions.

Lugones, M. (2003). *Pilgrimages/Peregrinajes: Theorizing Coalition Against Multiple Oppressions*. Lanham, MD: Rowman & Littlefield.

Mbembe, A. (2003). Necropolitics, *Public Culture*, 15(1), 11–40. doi:10.1215/08992363-15-1-11.

Mills, C. (2014). *Decolonising Global Mental Health: The Psychiatrization of the Majority World*. London: Routledge.

NHS Digital. *Mental Health Act Statistics, Annual Figures 2021–22*. London: NHS Digital, 2022. Available at: https://digital.nhs.uk/data-and-information/publications/statistical/mental-health-act-statistics-annual-figures/2021-22

Ramstead, M. J. D., Wiese, W. and Friston, K. J. (2022). Decolonizing psychiatry: Theory and practice. *Philosophy, Psychiatry, & Psychology*, 29(1), 45–65.

Rege, S. (2003). Dalit women talk differently: A critique of 'difference' and towards a Dalit feminist standpoint position. In: S. Rege (ed.), *Sociology of Gender: The Challenge of Feminist Sociological Knowledge*. New Delhi: SAGE, pp. 43–65.

Roberts, D. (2022). *Torn Apart: How the Child Welfare System Destroys Black Families—and How Abolition Can Build a Safer World*. New York: Basic Books.

Souza, L. A. (2021). Community mental health in Brazil: Lessons from CAPS. *Revista Brasileira de Saúde Mental*, 13(2), 1–18.

Spillers, H. J. (1987). Mama's baby, Papa's maybe: An American grammar book. *Diacritics*, 17(2), 65–81. doi:10.2307/464747.

Tuck, E. and Yang, K. W. (2014). R-words: Refusing research, In: D. Paris and M. T. Winn (eds.), *Humanizing Research: Decolonizing Qualitative Inquiry with Youth and Communities*. Thousand Oaks, CA: SAGE, pp. 223–248.

UK Government (2011). *Localism Act 2011: Chapter 20*. London: The Stationery Office.

Whyte, K. (2018). 'Indigenous science (fiction) for the Anthropocene: Ancestral dystopias and fantasies of climate change crises', *Environment and Planning E: Nature and Space*, 1(1–2), pp. 224–242.

Wynter, S. (2003). Unsettling the coloniality of being/power/truth/freedom: Towards the human, after man, its overrepresentation—An argument. *The New Centennial Review*, 3(3), 257–337.

Recommended further reading

Brah, (1996); Spivak, (1999); Anzaldúa, (1987) . *Strangers to Ourselves: Unsettled Minds and the Stories That Make Us*. New York: Farrar, Straus and Giroux.

A compelling examination of psychiatric diagnosis and identity through the lives of individuals navigating institutional and diagnostic boundaries.

Davidson, L. (2021). 'From Pipe Dream to Reality: A Practical Legal Approach Towards the Global Abolition of Psychiatric Coercion', in M. Bracken, L. Davidson and M. Gooding (eds) *Mental Health,*

Legal Capacity, and Human Rights. Cambridge: Cambridge University Press, pp. 147–177.

Proposes actionable legal frameworks for dismantling coercive psychiatric practices and replacing them with rights-based alternatives.

Fraiser-Carroll, M. (2023). *Mad World: The Politics of Mental Health*. London: Pluto Press.

An accessible introduction to Mad Studies that links mental health injustice with structural inequality, state violence, and neoliberal care regimes.

Jackson, B. (2025). *Fragile Minds: Stories from an NHS Mental Health Ward*. London: Jonathan Cape.

Acomposite account of life inside UK psychiatric wards, drawing attention to institutional neglect, systemic racism, and survivor resistance.

McGregor, L. (2023). *Detention and its Alternatives under International Law*. Oxford: Oxford University Press.

Acritical interrogation of carceral logics in mental health and international legal obligations to develop non-coercive care systems.

Epilogue: When silence becomes a weapon, so does the word Closing the door on reform, opening the path to insurgent healing

There is no neutral ground in the geography of psychiatric power. There are only those who disappear into it and those who return; the latter are not healed but hold fragments of truth that the state tried to erase.

Section 2 is more than a mechanism of detention. It is a necropolitical device, a gate through which the state enacts racialised control, silences dissent, and medicalises resistance. It is the hand of an empire in a white coat. It is grief recoded as disorder. It is rage pathologised into compliance.

Yet, in the shadows of that machinery, something else has always existed.

Survivors are not merely victims of psychiatric violence. They are its theorists. Its cartographers. Its disruptors. Through testimonial circles, sousveillance, and co-dreamed futures, they have already begun the work of abolition, not as an abstract idea but as a grounded, lived practice. In kitchens, gardens, encrypted group chats, and night-time vigils, they build care that does not punish and solidarity that does not surveil.

The CARE framework offered in this chapter – Community, Accountability, Relationality, Ecology – is not a programme. It is a refusal. A refusal to be measured by institutional metrics. A refusal to rehabilitate systems that were never meant to serve us. A refusal to be made legible through the diagnostic gaze.

But CARE is also a proposition: that we can organise our lives around reciprocity, not coercion; around kinship, not compliance. That healing can emerge from land, language, ritual, and rage. That memory itself can be a form of resistance.

To abolish Section 2 is not to create a void. It is to reclaim what that section stole: time, dignity, and autonomy, and the right to feel, to grieve, and to exist without being treated as a threat.

We are not calling for less aggression sedation or better cages. We are calling for a world without cages. A world where surveillance does not masquerade as protection. Where trauma is not criminalised. Where survival is not pathologised.

This is not utopia. It is already happening – in CAPS circles in Brazil, Ubuntu sanctuaries in South Africa, peer-led sessions in India, and here in the UK, in repurposed spaces where survivors are caring for each other because the system will not.

The revolution is not pending. It is in rehearsal.

And when the last seclusion room is closed, when no one is sectioned in the name of help, we will not look back to mourn psychiatry's undoing. We will look around – to lavender fields where restraint beds once stood, to communal kitchens where medication timetables once dictated life – and know:

We didn't wait.
We remembered the world.
We weren't restored.
We were reimagined.
We didn't heal the system.
We became the rupture.

Index

www.ingramcontent.com/pod-product-compliance
Ingram Content Group UK Ltd.
Pitfield, Milton Keynes, MK11 3LW, UK
UKHW022335201225
466288UK00009B/69

9 781915 271129